The Ultimate Prepper's Survival Bible

Your All-In-One Guide to Thriving in Any Crisis

Master Life-Saving Skills in Prepping, Food Storage, Water Filtration, Self-Defense, and More to Build a Secure and Self-Reliant Future

EVA GREENLEAF

Copyright © 2024 by EFKET LTD

All rights reserved.

No part of this publication may be reproduced, distributed, or transmitted in any form or by any means, including photocopying, recording, or other electronic or mechanical methods, without the prior written permission of the publisher, except as permitted by U.S. copyright law.

Disclaimer and Legal Notice:

The information contained in this book is for educational and informational purposes only and is not intended as medical or professional advice. The author and publisher are not responsible for any adverse effects or consequences resulting from the use of the information provided. Readers should consult with a qualified professional before undertaking any of the practices described in this book.

While every effort has been made to ensure the accuracy and completeness of the information provided, the author and publisher make no guarantees regarding the results obtained from the information contained in this book. The author and publisher expressly disclaim any liability for any loss or damage incurred as a result of the use or reliance on this book.

Some names, locations, and dates may have been changed for privacy reasons.

First Edition, 2024

Published by EFKET LTD

DEDICATED

To those who choose preparedness over fear and self-reliance over uncertainty

To the preppers who never stop learning and preparing for the unexpected

To those who strive to protect their loved ones in uncertain times

PREFACE

I was a total book nerd when I was a kid—loved reading adventure and survival stories to prepare myself for any challenging situations I might face in life. Little did I know that those skills would become incredibly handy later on!

Life is all about being prepared for whatever gets thrown your way, whether it's a freak blizzard, hurricane, or just running out of gas in the middle of nowhere. Stuff happens, and if you're not ready to handle it, you're up a creek without a paddle.

That's why I got into the prepper lifestyle—not because I'm a doomsday nut waiting for the apocalypse, but because I'm a regular person who'd rather be safe than sorry when it comes to caring for my family. As the saying goes, an ounce of prevention is worth a pound of cure.

I'm not a Rambo, but over the years, I've picked up a lot of tricks from scouting, camping, and reading survival manuals cover-to-cover. Skills like starting fires, filtering water, and even living off the land are invaluable.

After experiencing a terrifying moment in the mountains, I vowed to equip myself fully to survive. I learned amazing skills, like making fire using glasses from expert tutors, and how to locate potable water in unlikely places. We practiced making shelters out of leaves and branches, and learned to hunt and gather food from nature. We were shown which plants are edible and which are not, and how to set traps for food.

I also acquired specialized emergency medical care certifications, learning how to deliver medical aid, tie up fractures using only available materials, stitch deep wounds, and carry injured persons without worsening their condition. This first aid knowledge can mean the difference between life and death when help is far away.

Throughout my adolescence, I attended every available class, read every publication, and followed up with numerous practical trainings. I wanted to be 100% prepared for any insane tragedy that might occur, to protect myself and take care of my family. Those are the people who will survive!

That's why I wrote this book: to share what I've learned about keeping myself and my loved ones protected no matter what life throws at us. With simple instructions and my guides, you'll be prepared for any situation.

I'm an avid outdoorswoman who loves empowering people to be more self-reliant. If you'll let me, I'll ensure you have the tools to survive and thrive through any challenge in your life!

CONTENTS

PREFACE v

Introduction 13

Chapter 1 Build Your Survival Foundation 23

    Identify and Prioritize Potential Threats 23

    Assess Your Resources 24

        Exercise to Assess Resources 25

    Create a Personalized Survival Plan 27

        Preparing For Natural Disasters 28

        Hurricanes and Tropical Storms 28

        Tornadoes 29

        Earthquakes 29

        Wildfires 30

        Winter Storms and Extreme Cold 31

        Long-Term Food Storage 32

        Water Acquisition and Purification 33

    Prepare for Specific Scenarios 35

    Ensuring Continuity of Operations 38

    Build a Strong Survival Community 41

Chapter 2 Assemble Your Emergency Supply Kit 43

    Identify Your Needs 43

    Tools & Equipment 44

    What to Stock and How Much 45

    Estimate Your Food Needs 46

        Consider Budget-Friendly Options 48

        Practice Emergency Drills 49

        Skills to Become a Prepper 50

    Emergency Kits for Various Crisis Scenarios 52

Chapter 3 Mastering Food Preservation 55
Food Canning at Home 55
Shelf Life of Canned Foods 56
Methods of Food Preservation 56
Best Ways of Curing and Smoking 57
Dehydrate Foods for Long-Term Storage 57
Three Benefits of Dehydrating 58
Two Steps to Dehydrate Food 59
Two Dehydration Methods 60
Fermentation Techniques for Food Preservation 60
Benefits of Fermentation 61
Fermentation Methods 62
Practice Your Canning & Preserving Skills 63
Homegrown Food and Gardening 63
Hunting, Foraging, and Trapping 64
Home Fermentation Case Studies 69

Chapter 4 Ensuring Water Security 73
Create a Water Storage Plan 73
Purification Methods for Drinking 77
Harvest Rainwater 80
Utilize Alternative Water Sources 81

Chapter 5 Shelter and Security 85
Secure Your Home and Property 85
Step to Secure the Exterior of Your Home in Hurricane Crisis 87
Secure the Outer Layers 88
Defend Against other Dangers 92
Shelter Building Strategies 94
Bonus 98

Alternative Power and Energy 98
　　Renewable Power Generation 98
　　Backup Generators 99
　　Heating and Cooling 99
　　Power Storage and Conservation 100
　　Self-Defense Techniques 100

Chapter 6 Health and Wellness 105
　　Emergency Life-Saving Skills 105
　　First Aid Basics for Emergency Situations 106
　　　　Treating Burns 110
　　　　Splinting Broken Bones 110
　　　　Caring for Head Injuries 111
　　　　Dental Emergencies 114
　　　　Obstetrical Care 115
　　　　Patient Movement 115
　　Maintain Hygiene and Sanitation Standards 117
　　Being Prepared Can Save Lives 122

Chapter 7 Mobility And Evacuation Plans 127
　　Create Evacuation Routes And Rally Points 127
　　　　Map Your Area's Resources 129
　　　　Choose Rally Points 130
　　　　Route Planning Considerations 130
　　　　Practice Walking Routes 131
　　　　Pedestrian Evacuation Checklist 132
　　Vehicle Preparedness And Maintenance 133
　　　　Off-Road Capabilities 136
　　　　Emergency Fuel Storage 136
　　　　Electrical System Backups 137

    Emergency Communications 137

  Strategies for Surviving on the Move 140

    Foraging and Hunting Food 141

    Concealment and Camouflage 142

    Cryptic Communication 143

    Environmental Survival 143

Chapter 8 Financial Preparedness 147

  Economic Impact of a Crisis 147

  Manage Finances in Uncertain Times 150

  Barter and Trade in a Post-Disaster Economy 156

Chapter 9 Psychological Preparedness 161

  Coping Strategies for Stress and Anxiety 161

  Develop Resilience in Crisis Situations 166

  Maintain a Positive Mindset for Survival 171

Chapter 10 Herbal Medicine and Natural Remedies 175

  Use Medicinal Plants for Health and Healing 175

    Growing Your Medicinal Garden 176

    Wild Foraging for Medicinal Plants 178

    Medicinal Herbal First Aid Kit 178

  DIY Herbal Medicine Preparation Techniques 180

    Drying and Preserving Herbs 184

  Herbal Remedies for Common Ailments 185

    Herbal Remedies for Stomach Issues 186

    Herbal Remedies for Respiratory Issues 188

    Herbal Pain Relief Remedies 189

    Helping Cuts and Owies with Plants 190

Bonus Chapter Communication Strategies 193

  Establish Reliable Communication Channels 193

  Use Ham Radios and Other Communication Devices 194

Creative Ways to Send Messages 195

Set Up Home Communication Command Center 196

Set Up Community-Level Communication Networks 197

  Utilize other Emergency Communication Devices 201

  Set Up a Radio Watch Program 202

  Utilize Radio Repeaters 203

  Extending Your Radio's Capabilities 205

Coordinate with Emergency Services and Authorities 206

  Know Your Local Emergency Systems 207

  Prepping to Assist Responders 208

  Getting Certified to Assist 209

Conclusion 213

Bonus Extra Preparedness Toolkit 215

Continuing Education and Adaptation 217

Facing the Future with Confidence 218

References 221

Glossary 229

INTRODUCTION

Being a prepper is about preparing for emergencies and staying safe and strong during a crisis. Preppers don't panic; they plan to protect themselves and their families during tough times. By being prepared, they can face any crisis with confidence and peace of mind. This readiness isn't just smart—it's an act of love and care for the ones who matter most.

It's like how parents tell kids to pack an umbrella on a cloudy day in case it rains. Or how families bring snacks on road trips so they don't get hungry if stuck in traffic. We live in an unpredictable world where disasters like hurricanes, blizzards, and blackouts can strike out of nowhere. A true prepper understands that and prepares their family to handle such situations smoothly.

COVID-19 spread everywhere, showing how easily things we rely on can get messed up. Grocery stores ran out of food because people were buying way too much. Normal daily life got all shaken up. For some people, this was a wake-up call, a reminder to be prepared for unexpected events.

After COVID-19, people realised why preppers do what they do. They saw how being prepared can help during tough times, like having enough food and supplies at home. When stores ran out of supplies, it showed us how fast we could run out of what we needed. Lockdowns proved how quickly our regular lives can be disrupted, bringing everything to an abrupt halt. If something worse happens, being prepared could mean the difference between staying safe and struggling without a plan in a crisis.

The world can feel scary if you watch too much news. Climate change is making natural disasters worse. Political tensions are high. It can make people want to hide! But freaking out and panicking won't help anyone. The smarter approach is to calmly assess potential risks and create a clear plan to protect your loved ones, just in case.

That's where prepping comes in. It's not about overthinking worst-case scenarios. It's about feeling empowered to handle unpredictable situations confidently. Having the right skills, supplies, and mindset turns you from a victim into a prepared survivor.

Introduction

Nobody wants kids to go hungry or be unsafe just because the power went out after a storm. Prepping allows families to survive the disruptions and keep everyone safe when normal life gets disrupted.

At its core, prepping gives a lifestyle of readiness. You'll sleep better knowing you have backup plans for emergencies instead of winging it. That peace of mind makes the effort worth it.

This book will guide you on how to become a prepper. It outlines the things to put in the emergency kit, procedures to be followed, medical treatment essentials, and key things to know to safeguard you and your family in an emergency. In this book, you will discover the ability to be ready for any form of trouble life brings.

Importance of Preparation in Uncertain Times

Dealing with life's surprises can be tough. It's all about staying ready, keeping cool, making smart choices, and ensuring you can bounce back when things get rough.

People who prep are all about getting ready for emergencies because it's not just about stocking up on supplies. It's a commitment to keeping their loved ones safe in tough times.

Preppers gather stuff like food, water, and medicine but also learn how to grow food, use energy sources, give CPR, and more. Most importantly, they get themselves mentally, emotionally & financially ready to handle any emergency.

Their main aim is to be strong enough to look after themselves & their family if something goes wrong.

Resource Management

You need to be prepared for emergencies. It is important to support yourself and your family. Doing so will reduce the burden on public services and infrastructure. This will also help avoid the chaos of finding supplies at the last minute.

Informed Decision-Making

When things get tough, stress can make it hard to think clearly. But if you're ready, you can have a plan and the know-how to carry it out. This way, you can avoid making mistakes because of panic. Looking ahead like this is important for keeping people safe and protecting their stuff. It also helps folks react in a calmer and better way.

Community Resilience

When you and your family are all set, it doesn't just help you guys out - it's good for the whole bunch of people living near you. When everyone can care for themselves, emergency crews don't need to work as hard. Plus, they can lend a hand to neighbors who might need some help. By getting everyone ready like this, neighborhoods become stronger and more able to bounce back quickly after bad stuff happens.

Economic Stability

When disasters happen, they can mess up the economy big time. The smart ones who are ready can lower money problems by looking after their stuff, saving for emergencies, and having more than one way to make money. This planning helps them get back on their feet faster and have less stress over money during tough times.

Introduction

Mental and Emotional Health

Being prepared also helps with your mind and feelings. It lowers worries and stress caused by not knowing what might happen. Having a plan and the things you need brings peace, so you can confidently take uncertain times.

So, being ready means safety, security, and peace in a world where nothing is guaranteed. It's a smart strategy that builds strength, helps make better choices, brings people closer together, and keeps your wallet safe.

Understanding the Prepper Mindset

The general concept defended by preppers is preparation for various challenges and stability in the face of adversity. It is not dependent on 'fear' but on sound reasoning and rationality for the want of security and protection for oneself and the family. The people plan for tomorrow's adversity and prepare themselves accordingly. Hence, they are prepared whenever something occurs, unlike some people they are preparing for. This readiness enables them to confront any event or condition that may arise with confidence and coolness.

Preparing involves constantly mimicking similar situations; thus, you are ready when a real one comes. It is all about not waiting for something to go wrong, that is, reacting, but getting it right the first time. A prepper can be defined as an individual who is ready for a particular kind of trouble before the trouble occurs.

People who prepare themselves are not passive; they do not wait for the disaster to happen and do not think about how to respond. They know how to treat actors and conceive how to prevent or even stop them. Survivalists call for ways to reduce the blows of disastrous incidences on their lives.

Prepper's mindset is critical as it provides an individual with some level of control over their life; through this, people can feel safe. Feeling ready for disasters prevents one from developing high tension and stress when waiting for failure. In the event of a disaster, those who have prepared can react accordingly and do not give in to panic, which sometimes ensues when calamity strikes. This demeanor helps prevent one from feeling the heat when dealing with those crises.

The general idea of a prepper or 'prepper' culture and regime is based on self-sufficiency. This is because, as preppers, they dedicate time to acquiring knowledge and relevant resources not to have to rely on anyone or anything external. These are horticultural activities like planting, aeromedical, especially first aid, and special banking. This keeps them informed in real-time, thus reducing the degree of dependence they place on systems that are very likely to fail during an emergency.

The prepper also cultivates a culture of hardiness based on the best practices advocated in the preparation for Armageddon. It fosters its students to make necessary changes without growing rigid when confronting problems, making them resourceful. This resilience is very handy in ensuring that families and the societies they are located are safer and stable.

Therefore, the term 'prepper' refers to a person who takes practical precautions when facing a threat, acts ahead of time on their own accord, and manages or controls a given situation. That way, you can plan the future with lots and lots and lots of planning as you carry a can-do attitude.

Introduction

Skills and Knowledge You'll Gain

The Ultimate Prepper's Survival Bible is the best companion and guide in crises, preparing you to face any natural or artificial calamities or disasters. Some areas that can be taught include finding food, water, shelter, defense skills, communication, and others. You will acquire all the fundamental lessons concerning prepping in very simple, straightforward methods involving real-time challenges that may happen during calamities.

In this book, you will discover how to preserve and pack foods, purify water, grow food, maintain basic shelters, protect yourself and your home, and much more. Other skills are:

- Managing medical emergencies.
- Cleaning of the facilities.
- Trading of resources.
- Non-networked means of communication.

Begin now, irrespective of previous experience with autonomy procedures, using this outline as a precursor to enhancing self-reliant skills in the future.

By reading this book, you will gain a wealth of knowledge that will empower you to face even the most challenging situations. It provides a framework to adapt your skills to any conditions, whether your location, the dangers around you, or your needs. This easily understandable manual is a reference source and tool for self-empowerment and preparedness for crises, instilling a sense of confidence and security in you.

These elements should ensure this toolkit contains life-sustaining basics, crucial directions, a model emergency supply kit, checklists, sample plans, real-life survival stories, and detailed instructions. With the knowledge gathered and documented in this book, you have the key to shielding your family and enduring everything. With this book, follow the steps to proper security and liberation through the power of personal responsibility.

It emphasizes evaluating relevant risks, creating personalized action plans, and building physical and mental resilience. It highlights the importance of a unified survival community, where combined strengths create an unbreakable support network. With this easy-to-follow handbook, even a child can understand the lifestyle of being constantly prepared. Ready yourself for the journey ahead. You'll become the ultimate survivor, securing your safety and those dear to you.

Real World Case Studies

By studying past and current events, you can prepare yourself well. You'll be able to face the emergencies and conserve important resources such as food and water. You'll also focus on your mental and emotional health.

Hurricane Katrina

August 2005 saw Hurricane Katrina hit the United States Gulf Coast, especially New Orleans, Louisiana.

It caused a lot of destruction and flooding and is one of the most dangerous hurricanes the country has ever had.

Because they did not expect the storm to be so bad, many people could not get ready in time or left it too late. This meant that the levees around New Orleans had broken when the hurricane was over, and the city was underwater.

How people were affected by the event called into question how ready New Orleans (and the country) was for something like this to happen. For example, some things rescuers needed immediately — like enough food, drink, and medicine — had not been planned for. Other agencies who would normally have helped couldn't do their jobs because they were getting many calls for help.

To ensure that nothing like this ever happens again, we need to plan for everything – that is one of the things we learned from Katrina. This includes planning how everyone will get out safely if they need to. It's also important to have things like food and water already bought and saved in case stores are closed when we need them. People also need to decide where everyone can meet up again if something happens and how they will get in touch with each other then.

California Wildfires

In California, destructive wildfires are driven by drought and winds every year.

When the fire spreads rapidly, it becomes easy for residential areas to receive evacuation orders. Individuals must prepare themselves for immediate and safe evacuation.

Californians pack emergency kits with bottled water, canned food, clothes, files, and bandages in anticipation of wildfire-related emergencies during summer.

Evacuation procedure practice and preparedness are improved through mock exercises.

Introduction

Canning During World War II

Rationing made saving food resources for the war possible, even during World War Two. This is because families engaged in home canning to keep fruits, vegetables, and meat safe. In times when there was very little food, Canning played an important role in enhancing public food safety.

One way to ensure that canned food remains edible entails putting it in tightly closed jars, which are then heated up so that all bacteria perish under such high temperatures. The fact that canning gained popularity throughout the Second World War indicated how people should learn to depend on themselves for basic needs such as food and, therefore, be self-sufficient.

COVID-19 Pandemic

Due to the COVID-19 pandemic, there were sometimes scarce supplies for some food products within the grocery. Many individuals resorted to farming and putting into practice some ways of keeping food in other stores, topping healthier diets than before. Did you store too many greens and have nowhere to put them down? Well, freeze them or make your dehydrator because it's easy today! When people learn how to preserve food properly, they will throw away less and ensure that there is always enough to eat, even when everything goes wrong.

Flint Water Crisis

Flint, Michigan, encountered a health concern in 2014 following lead pollution of city water from the new supply system. Due to the changing water systems and sources, residents were exposed to dangerous lead levels in their drinking systems.

The Flint water crisis highlighted the inherent weaknesses of the current apparatus employed to oversee water supplies and emphasized the necessity for rigorously monitoring water quality. This made families use bottled water for survival purposes, showing that clean and dependable water is essential.

The Drought In Cape Town

The drought in Cape Town was one of the biggest water crises to befall Cape Town, South Africa, from 2017 to 2018. This resulted in enforced daily allocation for the citizens. Residents must adhere to strict weekly regimes or risk running totally off water. It highlighted the importance of sustainable measures of water conservation and management.

Japan Earthquake

> A strong earthquake hit Japan with an accompanying tsunami, leading to massive destruction and deaths in March 2011. Those who survived went through a lot of pain, losing loved ones, and they had to seek psychological support to be able to overcome the trauma. Mental health became a key issue across communities; they fostered support groups focused on trauma counseling and encouraged conversation about such issues to overcome them.

CHAPTER 1
BUILD YOUR SURVIVAL FOUNDATION

In this chapter, we will examine how to analyze your situation and prioritize potential dangers, evaluate what resources you have at your disposal, and devise a plan that considers both.

By understanding where you stand right now – figuratively speaking – it becomes possible to work out what actions are most important (and when) and use everything available more efficiently.

Whether you live in an area frequently buffeted by hurricanes, atop an earthquake fault line, or within spitting distance of several million people, this examination should inform how you prepare yourself: keeping safe and well as possible.

Building resilience upon firm foundations means thinking—sometimes well ahead—planning for different possibilities, and having confidence and competence in whatever (potentially awful) surprises life may bring.

I will show you how to develop such a strategy that does more than just readying yourself for extreme events but empowers day-to-day living with greater equanimity amid uncertainty: being prepared for anything while enjoying everything!

Identify and Prioritize Potential Threats

Should you wish to prepare for emergencies, which is the initial step that must be taken? Think in advance with a little thought about what could go wrong, including potential disastrous events in your locality that may affect people living there.

You can turn potential disasters into manageable challenges by considering and analyzing the circumstances, including identifying potential disasters. This will make sure that you are prepared for anything.

Ultimately, it's about transforming fear into confidence, ensuring you and your loved ones are ready to handle whatever comes your way. From fearing disasters to being prepared for them, this mindset shift empowers you to face uncertain times with resilience and calm.

1. List possible hazardous events, e.g., hurricanes and earthquakes.
2. Consider what else could arise during these events, e.g., a blackout or lack of commodities.

Chapter 1
Build Your Survival Foundation

> 3. Evaluate the risks depending on how likely they are to happen and how serious they would be.
>
> 4. Give priority to the risks you should prepare for and concentrate on preparing yourself for the least probable but most dangerous cases.

Consider the usual climatic conditions within your locality. Are blizzards, hurricanes, and tornadoes common? Is there any chance of experiencing drought or wildfire? Lastly, how susceptible is the place to flooding? If along a fault line, plan for earthquakes and volcanoes, too. Make a list of natural disaster threats requiring preparation.

But don't just think about nature's hazards. Also, look for man-made risks like chemical plants, rail lines with hazardous materials, or nuclear reactors nearby. Those facilities have emergency plans, but you should make your own.

Don't forget regular municipal risks like power outages, infrastructure failures, civil unrest, or supply chain disruptions. Even temporary road closures or strikes could leave you stuck without essentials.

Once you assess likely scenarios, prioritize prepping based on the chances and timing. For example, a two-week food and water supply makes sense for everyone. But if in a hurricane zone, create an evacuation plan and get a generator.

The goal is not to panic over every possible scenario. Otherwise, the most important thing that should be done is to honestly consider your position and then concentrate on those essential preparations that will help protect you and your family.

Assess Your Resources

It is essential that before deciding to take preventive measures against unexpected occurrences or calamity, consideration should be given to your inventory. There is a high chance that you may have a variety of important commodities and knowledge, which might play a big role in tackling hard times. This straightforward approach will ensure you know where to channel your energy by determining what you lack and don't in terms of strength or ability.

Step 1: What You Have

Prepare a catalog for anything that might be useful during an urgent situation. This should cover your financial resources, employment competencies, social network, domestic help, means of transportation, and information about where you live.

Assess Your Resources
The Ultimate Prepper's Survival Bible

Step 2: Your Advantages

Consider the possible benefits of your present circumstances. For instance, in your locality, there could be a well or you may have installed solar panels. Point out any possible advantages you can think of having right now.

Step 3: Existing Supplies

Take some time to survey your residence and note down all available emergency supplies, such as non-perishable food, camping gear, tools, and first aid kits. You likely possess more such fundamental survival commodities than you think.

Step 4: Your Living Space

Take time and carefully look at your living space. Note any characteristics within your environment that may be useful in an emergency, such as backup generators, green zones, proximity to water, etc., and readily available escape routes. It's important to point out some issues like congested spaces; what if there is no plan B for heating or cooling?

Only when you know what you possess and lack can you formulate a solution for filling those gaps. This may mean acquiring additional skills, purchasing more supplies, or modifying your house. However, do not just take another person's plan and put it as yours because you need something different specifically for yourself.

Exercise to Assess Resources

Step 1: What You Have

Category	Details
Physical Items	
Skills	
Financial Assets	
Support Network	
Other Resources	

Chapter 1
Build Your Survival Foundation

Step 2: Your Advantages

Current Living Situation Advantages	Other Personal Advantages

Step 3: Existing Supplies

Category	Details
Food Supplied	
Medical Supplies	
Tools and Equipment	
Emergency Supplies	

Create a Personalized Survival Plan
The Ultimate Prepper's Survival Bible

Category	Details
Other Supplies	

Step 4: Your Living Space

Helpful Features	Potential Problems

Create a Personalized Survival Plan

Having assessed the possible dangers, you keep stock of what is there or what you have. So now gather everything discussed earlier about your situation and put it into a personalized emergency plan for yourself.

This program should consider certain elements surrounding you; these may include but are not limited to the favorable risk events identified by the agent, as well as your strengths and weaknesses. Designing this plan will ensure that you cover every important part and give you confidence in your ability to act effectively during difficult times because of its customized nature.

Chapter 1
Build Your Survival Foundation

Preparing For Natural Disasters

The part has information on what to do if there are natural calamities in your region. It looks at typical tragedy types and ways of preparing for them. Planning for potential hazards around your environment is crucial because nobody can be completely ready for anything that may come their way.

Hurricanes and Tropical Storms

People residing on the coast must be prepared for hurricanes. Here are some important steps to take:

Checklist Item	Actions
Check home's resilience to strong winds, floods, and storm surges	Assess your home's ability to withstand these conditions based on location and construction.
Install hurricane shutters or cover windows with plywood	Secure windows using hurricane shutters or plywood to protect against wind and debris.
Secure outdoor items and reinforce external doors.	Ensure loose outdoor items are tied down and reinforce external doors to prevent them from being damaged by wind.
Monitor storm trajectory and follow evacuation orders	Stay informed about the storm's path and promptly evacuate if authorities issue evacuation orders.
Prepare supplies and essential documents.	Gather sandbags, emergency food, and important documents to have them ready in case of evacuation or emergency.

During the storm, all family members should shelter in the innermost room, basement, or specially-designed safe room until all clear.

Post-hurricane, be prepared for temporary displacement, lack of power, clean water, and dealing with heavy debris: tools, tarps, chainsaws, and other gear on hand aid recovery.

Create a Personalized Survival Plan
The Ultimate Prepper's Survival Bible

Tornadoes

The lightning-fast impacts of tornadoes demand their dedicated preparedness plan, especially in "Tornado Alley" regions. Key considerations include:

Checklist Item	Actions
Install an underground storm shelter or safe room	Construct or install a shelter underground or a reinforced safe room.
Understand tornado warning systems and sirens.	Learn about different tornado warning systems and how sirens work.
Teach family members proper sheltering techniques.	Educate all family members on the correct procedures for taking shelter during a tornado.
Avoid windows and doors, shelter under heavy furniture if needed	Avoid windows and doors; seek shelter under sturdy furniture if necessary.
Prepare shoes, hard hats, and protective gear.	Keep shoes, hard hats, and other protective equipment readily available during a tornado emergency.

Be prepared for catastrophic damage afterward, requiring sheltering elsewhere until all debris is cleared. Medical kits for severe injuries are a must as well.

Earthquakes

Living in areas prone to earthquakes means you need to have good plans and supplies ready for when an earthquake happens. Here are some things you should have:

Checklist Item	Actions
Emergency backpack with	Prepare a backpack containing food, water, a radio, and other

Chapter 1
Build Your Survival Foundation

essentials	essentials that can be quickly grabbed during an emergency.
Secure heavy furniture and items	Ensure that heavy furniture, shelves, and items are properly secured to prevent them from falling or causing injury during an earthquake.
Prepare for fires	Have fire extinguishers and tools ready to shut off utilities to prevent fire hazards and damage after an earthquake.
Identify safe spots for cover.	Identify safe areas away from windows and exterior walls where you can cover during an earthquake.
Plan exit strategies	Determine alternative exit routes or options to leave the premises safely if the building becomes structurally unsafe after an earthquake.
Establish multiple communication methods.	Set up various communication methods to reach family members and check others' safety during and after an earthquake.

Wildfires

Wildfires are becoming a year-round danger because of climate change. Here are some important tips to stay safe:

Checklist Item	Actions
Maintain defensible space	Clear brush and vegetation around your property to create a buffer zone that helps protect your home from wildfires.
Use fire-resistant materials	Invest in fire-resistant building materials, and consider enclosing eaves to prevent embers from entering your home.
Install an exterior fire sprinkler system.	If you live in a high-risk wildfire zone, consider installing an exterior fire sprinkler system to protect your home during a fire.
Prepare go-bags and evacuation routes.	Pack emergency go-bags in advance with essentials and map out evacuation routes to quickly leave the area if needed.

Create a Personalized Survival Plan
The Ultimate Prepper's Survival Bible

Protect against smoke	Have respirators, masks, and goggles on hand to protect yourself from smoke during a wildfire.
Plan temporary housing arrangements.	Pre-plan temporary housing options if you need to evacuate and cannot return home immediately after a wildfire.

Winter Storms and Extreme Cold

Strong winter storms and cold events show that preparing for winter is just as important as getting ready for hurricanes in certain areas. Some key steps to take are:

Checklist Item	Actions
Insulate and weatherproof home exterior.	Ensure your home's exterior is well-insulated and weatherproofed to keep it warm and protected from harsh weather conditions.
Stockpile heating fuel, wood, and warm clothing.	Gather enough heating fuel, firewood for the fireplace, and warm clothing to stay comfortable during cold weather and potential power outages.
Install carbon monoxide and fire detectors.	Install carbon monoxide and smoke detectors and clean chimneys to prevent fire hazards and monitor air quality.
Prepare for power and supply disruptions.	Be ready for potential power outages and disruptions in supply chains by stocking up on essentials and having alternative energy sources available.
Have backup generators and solar chargers.	Ensure access to backup generators and solar chargers to keep devices powered in case of electricity loss during snowstorms.
Secure snow removal equipment	Keep snow removal equipment like shovels and salt on hand to clear driveways and walkways for safe passage during heavy snowfall.
Ability to stay put for extended periods	If snowed in, prepare to stay indoors for extended periods by stocking up on food, water, medications, and other necessities.

This prepper guide helps people be prepared for any seasonal risks specific to their location,

Chapter 1
Build Your Survival Foundation

ensuring they are always ready for the worst that nature can bring.

Long-Term Food Storage

Preppers prioritize building a large stock of shelf-stable foods that can sustain their family long without needing more supplies from outside. Typically, they aim to have enough food to last at least one year.

Checklist Item	Actions
Stock bulk shelf-stable foods	Gather rice, wheat, oats, dehydrated and freeze-dried meals, canned goods, powdered milk, powdered eggs, and more.
Include fats, oils, and nut butter.	Add fats and oils like olive oil, coconut oil, and nut butter to provide essential healthy fats.
Store beans, lentils, and split peas	For protein and fiber, keep a supply of beans, lentils, and split peas.
Ensure multivitamins and supplements.	Include multivitamins and supplements to meet nutritional needs over a long period.
Choose calorie-dense and nutrient-rich foods.	Prioritize foods that are hearty, calorie-dense, and provide essential nutrients like proteins and complex carbs.
Use proper storage methods.	Store food in cool, dark, dry places in airtight containers with oxygen absorbers and desiccants to prevent spoilage.
Rotate and replace stock regularly.	Regularly use and replace older stock to ensure freshness and prevent food from worsening.

Create a Personalized Survival Plan
The Ultimate Prepper's Survival Bible

| Implement gardening, farming, and animal husbandry. | Develop gardening, farming, and raising animals skills to create a sustainable food source for long-term needs. |

Store bulk items such as rice, wheat, oats, dehydrated and freeze-dried meals, canned goods, powdered milk, powdered eggs, fats, oils, nut butter, honey, beans, lentils, split peas, multivitamins, and supplements.

The key is choosing hearty, calorie-dense foods that can last long when stored properly. These foods contain complete proteins, healthy fats, complex carbs, and important nutrients. To avoid spoilage, the food must be packed in airtight containers containing oxygen absorbers or desiccants and kept at low temperatures away from sunlight and moisture. Preppers also regularly use and replace older stock to prevent it from worsening.

Preppers are known for their various ways of ensuring that food does not run out, including gardening, farming, and keeping animals, all of which guarantee a continuous food supply even in hard times.

Water Acquisition and Purification

The next necessary item for storage, following food, is water, which should be obtained from different sources and in plenty. This forms a very important section of this survivalist manual.

Checklist Item	Actions
Store clean drinking water in containers.	Use strong containers for long-term water storage to store clean drinking water.
Develop self-reliant water resupply methods.	Set up methods for continually accessing fresh water, such as digging wells with hand pumps or collecting rainwater.
Use filtration and purification systems.	Implement filtration systems to remove impurities and know how to purify contaminated water from various sources.
Locate underground springs or set water traps.	Scout for underground springs or set traps to catch water from natural sources.
Have reliable backup power	Solar panels or other backup power sources operate water

Chapter 1
Build Your Survival Foundation

sources.	filtration and purification systems.
Stock up on portable water filters and purifiers.	Acquire portable water filters and purifiers to treat unsanitary water sources when needed.
Accumulate chlorine tablets and purification supplies.	Stockpile chlorine tablets and other purification supplies to ensure water safety during emergencies.
Maintain a multi-layered approach to ensure hydration.	Implement a combination of water storage, self-reliant water collection methods, and purification technologies.

Initially, there should be a good supply of clean drinking water kept in safe, long-lasting containers. Nonetheless, this is just a stop-gap measure.

Preppers go the extra mile to ensure they always have clean drinking water. These include installing hand pumps, rainwater collectors, and filtration systems, among other ways of gathering water.

They also understand how to treat contaminated water and can use even natural sources to purify it. In addition, preppers may find underground springs or set traps for catching water.

This is where having dependable solar power and filtering or purifying stagnant water comes in handy. They need to stock up on chlorine tablets and other purification equipment. Therefore, their multiple strategies help secure enough drinking supplies during crises such as failure in the normal water system.

Prepare for Specific Scenarios

The sad truth is that calamities and unforeseen events can occur unpredictably, even if you have made arrangements for them and are fully prepared. One may face a personal emergency when everything seems okay, and one is not prepared enough due to some freak accident, criminal act, etc. Often, an isolated individual requires certain aptitudes to overcome such cases.

It does not matter the extent of training that someone has undergone as long as it is geared towards helping them deal with dangerous situations in which they might be alone, without help from the police or society.

Having the right equipment is crucial, but what matters most is applying what you know and your skills and staying calm when things get tough.

Preppers in tough situations like wilderness isolation, violent encounters, or major disasters rely on their skills to survive dangerous challenges. Their ability to adapt and stay strong is crucial for survival.

The following individual scenarios show how the prepper mindset provides the critical thinking, physical capability, and mental strength to survive and overcome some of the most scary challenges possible when the odds seem undefeatable:

Crisis 1: Stranded in the Desert

Suppose you were driving across the desert southwest when your car broke down on a remote stretch of road. You have no cell signal, limited supplies, and the nearest town is over 50 miles away through harsh, unforgiving land.

Step 1: Use Your Kit

With the prepper mindset and training, you remain calm instead of panicking. You must have essentials in your trunk's emergency kit, like water, energy bars, essential tools, warm clothing, fire starters, and a detailed map.

Step 2: Use your Navigation Skills

Using the map and your navigation skills, you position yourself and plan a safe route, marking potential dangers like sandy basins or rocky outcroppings to avoid. You limit how much water you drink and use sunlight to collect more water from condensation.

Step 3: Your Safety

You create a small fire for signaling and make a makeshift shelter to shade from the strong sun. At night, you stay warm and avoid hypothermia by burning whatever combustible material you

Chapter 1
Build Your Survival Foundation

can search for, following proper firecraft and safety.

You get rescued after three tiring days of walking through the desert when you finally come across a rural petrol station.

Crisis 2: Home Invasion

At night, some people carrying weapons invade your home in search of money. They appear like they are very much in need and can cause harm to you.

Step 1: The Must-Haves

Fortunately, your preparedness measures for security are triggered straight away. There is a safe enclosure in which you have installed heavy-duty locks plus some CCTV so that you may examine what is happening around you.

Step 2: Grab the Protective Gears

You take some safety equipment from this place of fear, such as bulletproof jackets and gun spares.

Step 3: Call for Help

In case of an emergency, you would waste no time but seek assistance while at the same time ensuring that your neighbors are aware through the use of some communication gadgets for emergencies, such as radios and signal mirrors. You ration food supplies and drinking water very prudently. Non-lethal weapons like pepper spray are there with you in case they are needed to scare away any attackers who may attempt to break into your place. And if all else fails, you can access guns and tactical gear, which are properly stored.

You stand your ground throughout the night, and finally, the intruders run off when they see that overcoming you is not easy at all. Your strong home security and preparedness allow you to survive this frightening situation without hurting anyone.

Crisis 3: Wilderness Injury

While camping far from help, your friend breaks a bone badly, with a bone sticking out and a lot of bleeding. You're miles away from any trailhead or camp.

Step 1: Stop the Bleeding

Using wilderness first aid skills, you immediately make a tourniquet with a strap and trekking pole to stop heavy bleeding. Next, you support and protect the broken bone to avoid more harm. You give pain relief medicine from your stocked first aid kit.

Step 2: Use your GPS Device

You get into your emergency shelter, keeping your partner warm and safe, making sure he can breathe easily. You send a distress signal for help using your GPS device, giving your exact location for rescue.

<u>Step 3: Be Consistent</u>

Throughout the next 12 hours, you continue providing medical aid while creating signal fires and hanging bright markers on surrounding trees to assist rescuers in locating you quickly.

Your expertise in navigation and field medicine helps stabilize the situation until a helicopter arrives for evacuation, ensuring you are safely airlifted to a secure location.

Crisis 4: Kidnapping

While traveling abroad, if criminals kidnap you for ransom. They can keep you in a hidden place with bad conditions, little food, and water.

<u>Step 1: Keeping Calm</u>

Your training helps you stay calm and focused instead of getting scared. You watch your surroundings carefully, looking for any chances to escape.

<u>Step 2: Using Ingenuity</u>

Even with limited resources, you use your creativity to make tools. You might use things like hairpins or dental floss to unlock your restraints. Learning some of your captors' language can also help you connect with them.

<u>Step 3: Seizing the Opportunity</u>

When you see a good chance, you put your skills into action. You might disable one of your captors and escape when it's dark. Using what you've learned about survival, you stay free for days and find a way to reach a safe place like an emergency consulate.

Crisis 5: House Fire

An electrical fire breaks out in your home's basement, quickly filling it with thick smoke. Your family is trapped inside as flames spread rapidly.

<u>Step 1: Swift Action Response</u>

When you're prepared for emergencies, you can act quickly to address the situation. You immediately use pre-positioned fire extinguishers to put out the fire while it's still manageable. At the same time, someone in your family activates emergency respirator masks from your safety kit.

Chapter 1
Build Your Survival Foundation

<u>Step 2: Planned Evacuation</u>

As the fire grows beyond control, your practiced evacuation plan kicks in. You move to your specially reinforced bedroom's safety zone, which seals off from the smoke. Afterward, you could leave through a special emergency escape window fitted on the rooftop of your house.

<u>Step 3: Organized Response</u>

You will use the rope ladder, which is safe and secure, to descend. Afterward, you follow the normal fire escape procedures and get down safely. You gather everybody within the compound to ensure their safety when you touch the ground. In your efforts to keep your house safe, you also employ firefighting apparatus such as hoses and fire extinguishers up until the time when professional help arrives.

These tips could save your life in a hazardous disaster if observed well by a "prepper." It matters a lot; hence, one should stay composed and remember the basic ways of survival, then put them into action.

It is not enough for people who follow a prepper lifestyle to just gather supplies for the end of the world as we know it scenarios; being independent and competent in dealing with potential fatalities is essential. Preparedness involves having the ability to confront and overcome serious difficulties or dangerous crises of any kind.

Ensuring Continuity of Operations

In a time of crisis, should public service fail at the local level, then heads of districts are responsible for maintaining order and continuity through the following ways:

Checklist Item	Actions
Assign important job roles and tasks to specific people	Delegate specific responsibilities and tasks to individuals within the group.
Manage resources and establish backup plans for supplies	Monitor resources and develop contingency plans for acquiring additional supplies if needed.
Prioritize needs and address critical issues first	Determine the most urgent needs and prioritize addressing them promptly.
Conduct regular maintenance to ensure functionality.	Perform routine checks and maintenance to keep equipment and systems operational.

Ensuring Continuity of Operations
The Ultimate Prepper's Survival Bible

| Plan for future scenarios requiring extensive preparation | Develop long-term plans to prepare for potential future situations. |

In essence, preppers form little autonomous societies that ensure the functionality of their larger communities once central leadership fails.

Take a paper and list important matters after dividing them into key sections. For instance:

Aspect	Checklist Items
Shelter	• Secure your home's structure • Prepare a temporary evacuation location • Design an ideal living setup
Food and Water	• Stockpile food supplies • Harvest rainwater • Grow food • Hunt game
Medical	• Obtain medical training • Gather medical guides and equipment • Store medicine and supplies • Plan for improvised medical solutions
Power and Heat	• Identify alternative cooking methods • Secure lighting sources • Plan for temperature control without electricity • Prepare energy backups and fuel storage

Chapter 1
Build Your Survival Foundation

Safety and Security	<ul><li>Learn self-defense strategies</li><li>Establish conflict avoidance procedures</li><li>Implement operational security measures</li><li>Secure your perimeter</li><li>Protect your team from threats during breakdowns</li></ul>

No area should be taken lightly without honing skills and accumulating equipment over time in every part. Stay on course because if anything happens that could have been prevented and leads to loss of lives, then it would be a great tragedy!

Nevertheless, do not attempt to transform yourself into an all-out survivalist instantaneously. The best thing is that you should move from one point to another while giving priority to the key ones. Utilize technology, learn in class, join associations, and learn more ways to depend on yourself.

Don't forget that preparing can't make your family entirely safe from unforeseen circumstances. Instead, it provides flexibility and a strong foundation to recover and adapt smoothly during disruptions.

By creating a solid personalized action plan, you take control of your destiny instead of just hoping for the best when disaster strikes. This proactive approach brings invaluable peace of mind.

Build a Strong Survival Community

Movies make it seem romantic for one person to survive alone in the wild. But to be safe during a big crisis, you must be part of a strong community that works well together.

Strength in Numbers

Going alone means you'll get overwhelmed quickly. You'll be taking on too many risks by yourself and missing out on important resources and skills that others in a group can provide. A well-built team where everyone's role helps the others has a much better chance of making it through.

Build the Right Team

That's why prepper families start building their survival community early on. They carefully choose trustworthy members who share their values and have skills that fit well together. They also look for people whose personalities can handle stressful situations.

Distribute Responsibility

The group sets up reliable ways to communicate with each other. They also make sure everyone is accountable and that a clear leader and chain of command is established upfront.

From there, the group works efficiently to prepare for every possibility without doing redundant or overlapping work.

Some members focus on protection and security, while others take on special jobs like medical care, building things, getting supplies, childcare and education, spiritual support, etc. This ensures everyone's particular skills get used properly.

Pooling Resources

They also pool their resources by creating multiple stashes of emergency supplies like long-term food storage, ammunition, gear, and equipment. Having supplies spread out in different locations reduces the risk of losing everything.

Backup Plans

The group also develops safe houses and bugout locations in case they ever need to evacuate from their main base in an emergency.

The ultimate goal is to build an independent modern "tribe" that can operate separately from normal society if needed. But they still combine all their abilities so that no one gets left behind or falls through the cracks.

Chapter 1
Build Your Survival Foundation

Understand The True Meaning of Readiness

Surviving any actual worst-case scenario requires the human resources, expertise, and unified supportive spirit of an entire community working as a team.

Having that embedded network you can rely on gives you strength, resilience, and hope when facing the worst situations.

A strong, prepared tribe transforms preppers into real survivors who can endure crises by having each other's backs through any obstacle. Your readiness is at its peak.

To be prepared effectively, a complete evaluation of your case helps establish a firm foundation. It is possible to develop a customized plan for dealing with all aspects of your situation and take into consideration some specific requirements if you will identify the risks properly and evaluate what you have now in terms or materials and money, among other resources.

By comparing identified threats and current property, one can develop measures that will guarantee safety for both you and the parties involved. Such measures would ensure that despite any tragedy or catastrophe, you remain strong enough to overcome it because you will know how best you can utilize the available environment and material resources towards solving the problems on hand.

We covered the essential survival mindset and skills needed to make it through any situation. But now it's time to talk supplies. Having the fitting emergency kit stocked and ready is critical. That vital base of operations helps all those survival techniques work. In this next chapter, I'll guide you through assembling the ultimate bugout bag and supply stash.

CHAPTER 2
ASSEMBLE YOUR EMERGENCY SUPPLY KIT

Emergencies can occur suddenly, day or night. Fires, power outages, injuries - these are frightening experiences! However, if you make plans, there is no reason for your family to fear. It is a smart decision to construct an emergency storage kit. Don't forget to include food, water, medical supplies, and important equipment in the kit.

That way, you're prepared for anything that comes your way. Stay indoors when it's unsafe and go through! With your preparedness, you only have to sit at home comfortably riding off the event. The peace of mind comes when one has all the necessary commodities nearby. Ready for anything, you will face all comers comfortably with your kit intact.

Preppers know that it is better to prepare than panic. Having essential commodities in your emergency storage will relax you because you'll know they're all alright even when everything seems upside down.

You can stay safely at home using what you've kept instead of going on dangerous trips looking for more. If help is on its way and you depend on your resources, you won't cause trouble by consuming theirs!

By collecting proper gear, unlike most people doing nothing but running around. While many people will rush to stores during emergencies and deplete shared resources before long, being ready prevents one from being caught off guard without any course.

Identify Your Needs

Considering what your family requires and the likely dangers depending on where you live is crucial before assembling the kit. For example, in a countryside homestead, one will not need materials similar to those used in a three-bedroom flat within town.

Start by looking at how many people are in your family and if anyone has special dietary restrictions or medical needs. An infant will require different stockpile items than a teenager. The same goes for diabetics, elderly folks, or those with allergies. Make a list covering everyone's essentials.

Next, analyze what types of disasters are most likely to affect your area based on the climate, geography, and other risk factors discussed in Chapter 1. Living in a wildfire country means factoring in respirator masks and fire protection gear. Those in hurricane zones better have evacuation supplies included.

Chapter 2
Assemble Your Emergency Supply Kit

Tools & Equipment

These real-life examples demonstrate the tools needed for specific crises and how a prepper's mindset helps them think, stay strong, and overcome daunting challenges even when the odds seem impossible.

House Flood

A nearby creek overflowed during heavy rains, causing rapid flooding in your neighborhood. Suddenly, knee-deep brown water fills your home's lower level. It's an emergency, but your prepared supply kit has what you need to manage.

Tools Needed:

Item	Purpose
Safety goggles	Protect eyes from pollutants in floodwater.
Rubber hip waders	Allow wading through water without getting wet.
Heavy-duty gloves	Protect hands while moving soaked items.
Portable water purifier	Ensure clean drinking water.
Sanitation accessories	Maintain hygiene to prevent sickness.
Small solar power bank	Keep communication devices charged for updates.

With these tools, you can safely navigate through the flood, move belongings to higher ground, and ensure access to clean water and communication. This preparation means your family isn't stranded. When the waters recede, you'll be ready to restart and clean up without further trouble.

Winter Storm

Consider an unexpected snowstorm that buries all under twenty-four inches of snow, blocking roads and preventing the flow of electricity. You are very cold at home because there is no heating as a result of the blackout, and this may continue for some days.

You must take quick action and get prepared with some important items to remain safe.

Tool	Purpose
High-efficiency wood-burning stove	Provides indoor heating without electricity
Thermal jackets	It keeps you warm by retaining body heat
Insulated coverall suits	Adds extra layers for warmth
Heavy-duty shovels	Clears snow from pathways and around doors
Roof rakes	Removes snow from roofs to prevent damage and leaks

You will need these things to put the wood-burning stove on so that you can maintain a warm, snug environment in your house. Dress warmly with thermal coats and insulated coveralls to ensure you are comfortable and snug. Use strong shovels for opening ways and thick snow pile remover to avoid accumulation at the top level of your roofs.

It's all about being safe and warm before improvement arrives when you've planned out well with these key items for an emergency this winter.

What to Stock and How Much

During crises, there may not be enough food. However, taking appropriate measures means that the family will be cared for in terms of food. It would be best to consider hoarding non-perishable foods such as canned products, dehydrated foodstuffs, and freeze-dried meals.

Estimate the quantities suitable for your relatives. Preparedness will keep you from experiencing hunger pangs.

Supply Shortage

Empty grocery shelves reveal that the food supply chain was interrupted. Numerous households might go hungry over the next few weeks. But there's no need to stress about your family.

For a while now, you've been gathering foods that will last long, such as dried beans, rice, wheat flour, canned soup, or even tea and coffee bags. right… oh! Not forgetting those expensive freeze-packed stuff that stay edible until it hits its quarter century.

While others panic over the lack of food, your family can remain calm, knowing you have enough food stored for months.

Chapter 2
Assemble Your Emergency Supply Kit

You can easily prepare hearty, nutritious meals anytime. As the food shortage worsens before it improves, you can even share some of your surplus with neighbors or others in need without compromising your provisions. Early preparation ensures your loved ones will not go hungry during this crisis.

When it comes to edible essentials, you'll want a diverse mix of storage-friendly options, including:

Type of Food	Description	Storage Recommendation
Canned Goods	Includes vegetables, fruits, broths, and meats: nutrient-dense and high-calorie options with long shelf life.	Store in a cool, dry place
Dried Goods	Pasta, rice, grains, oats, cereals, flour, beans, and lentils. Lightweight and require only water to prepare.	Keep airtight containers in a cool, dry location.
Freeze-Dried Meals	Lightweight packets of freeze-dried entrees with a long shelf life. Reconstitute with hot water for quick meals.	Store in airtight containers in a cool, dry place
Powdered Milk/Eggs	Versatile dairy substitutes for baking and cooking.	Keep airtight containers in a cool, dry location.
Hard Candies/Nuts	Dense, compact calories are ideal for snacking and quick energy boosts.	Store in airtight containers in a cool, dry place
Supplements	Multivitamin reserves to supplement potential nutritional deficiencies.	Store in a cool, dry place

Estimate Your Food Needs

How much of those supplies should you stockpile? The general rule is to stash enough calorically dense food and water for each household member to survive at least two full weeks without resupply.

Realistically, many preppers aim to have at least a month's worth of provisions cached, with

Estimate Your Food Needs
The Ultimate Prepper's Survival Bible

some hardcore "doomsday" preppers squirreling away 6-12 months or more of essentials.

Figure that the average adult will require around 2,000-2,500 calories daily from a balance of proteins, carbs, fats, and nutritious fruits/veggies. Depending on age and activity level, kids can get 1,400-2,000 calories daily.

With that basic framework in mind, you can start calculating precise quantities based on your household size, factoring in a 25% buffer for safety. Make a master checklist tracking everything from shelf-stable protein sources to supplementary snacks, condiments, cooking oils, and electrolyte-replenishing beverages.

Other Factors to Consider

Having all the gear in the world doesn't matter much if it's not properly stored and organized for rapid access when you most need it. Smart preppers follow some basic protocols:

Step	Description	Example	Importance
Centralized Location	Dedicate a secure, climate-controlled space for preps to prevent degradation and ease inventory.	Basement, storm cellar, large closet	Protects supplies and aids inventory
Airtight Containment	Use heavy-duty containers to protect against moisture, pests, and contamination.	Plastic totes, watertight ammo cans	Preserves quality of supplies
Visible Labeling	Label containers with contents, quantities, and expiration dates; consider color-coding systems	Labeling system, color-coded labels	Facilitates quick identification and inventory
Prioritize Accessibility	Keep critical equipment easily accessible for quick retrieval during emergencies.	Place essentials upfront, clear pathways	Ensures readiness and efficiency in emergencies
Conduct Regular Audits	Regularly check and rotate supplies, restock low items, and replace soon-to-expire provisions.	Inventory checks, restocking schedule	Ensures freshness and readiness of supplies

Chapter 2
Assemble Your Emergency Supply Kit

Consider Budget-Friendly Options

When preparing your emergency supplies, consider budget-friendly options to maximize your resources without compromising quality. Prioritize essential items and consider bulk purchasing, discounts, or DIY solutions to stay within your budget.

Buy in Bulk

Purchasing bulk quantities of non-perishable food from big box stores or joining bulk buy clubs incredibly saves retail prices. Split oversized packages with friends to make it more affordable.

Hunt for Sales

Watch for case lot sales, closeouts, discontinued items, etc. Stock up when staple goods like rice, beans, canned veggies, and first aid supplies are discounted.

Try Dehydrating

Invest in an essential dehydrator and make your tray-stable food from sale produce and meats. It's way cheaper than freeze-dried survival meals.

Grow Your Own

Do you have a green thumb? Grow calorie crops like potatoes and squash to increase your stockpile for little to no cost. Learn food preservation skills, too.

Shop Used

Scour second-hand stores, garage sales, and online marketplaces for gently used hiking/camping gear, tools, books, and other prepper supplies someone else no longer needs.

DIY Where Possible

Many critical items permit do-it-yourself construction to cut costs without sacrificing quality or performance. Get handy!

Prioritize High Value

If funds are very tight, start by getting the most valuable, versatile goods that give you the biggest preparedness bang for your buck.

Build Gradually

You don't need everything all at once. Make a long-term plan spanning months or years to steadily accumulate preps without going broke.

Estimate Your Food Needs
The Ultimate Prepper's Survival Bible

Practice Emergency Drills

That's just the beginning once you've gathered the necessary supplies for emergencies. It's important to practice and test your preparations with real-life drills. Many people overlook this crucial step in being truly prepared for emergencies.

Activity	Description	Key Components
Fire Drills	Conduct recurring fire drills for household evacuation to designated rally points, including surprise nighttime scenarios.	Rapid evacuation and accountability
Shelter Set Up	Practice setting up emergency shelters (e.g., tents) quickly without instructions, ensuring all components are present—efficient setup of shelter systems.	Preparedness
Water Procurement	Test water purification systems and methods for accessing, transporting, and storing potable water. Water purification and storage verification	Resource management
Cooking and Sanitation	Rotate cooking duties over campfires, practice building and using improvised latrines, and Improvise cooking and sanitation techniques.	Survival skills
First Aid Challenges	Quiz family members on basic first aid procedures for burns, joint injuries, CPR, etc. First aid knowledge and response testing	Medical emergency skills
Day/Night Navigation	Conduct practice hikes navigating varied terrain using a map and compass for wayfinding Navigation and orientation in different conditions.	Outdoor navigation skills
Communication Tests	Test signaling equipment and emergency communication pathways with regional teams quarterly. Communication equipment and protocols testing	Emergency communication

Chapter 2
Assemble Your Emergency Supply Kit

Skills to Become a Prepper

At a minimum, responsible preppers should continually work on deepening their expertise across core domains like:

Food Acquisition & Preservation

Skill	Description	Purpose
Gardening/Permaculture	Growing food in gardens using sustainable methods that work with nature	Provide fresh food sustainably
Foraging & Hunting	Finding wild edible plants and animals to supplement your food supply	Gather additional food from natural sources
Canning/Dehydrating/Smoking	Preserving food by sealing it in jars, drying it, or smoking it to extend shelf life	Store food long-term for future consumption
Plant & Mushroom Identification	Recognizing safe-to-eat plants and mushrooms and identifying those that are harmful or toxic	Avoid consuming dangerous plants and fungi.

First Aid & Sanitation

Skill	Description	Purpose
Herbal Remedies	Using plants to treat common ailments and illnesses	Natural alternative to conventional medicine
Wound Treatment	Cleaning and dressing wounds properly to prevent infection	Promotes healing and prevents complications
Pathology Diagnosis	Recognizing signs and symptoms of illness or disease	Early detection and appropriate medical response

Estimate Your Food Needs
The Ultimate Prepper's Survival Bible

| Hygiene & Waste Management | Maintaining cleanliness and proper disposal of waste to prevent contamination | Prevents spread of disease and maintains sanitation |

Bushcraft & Fieldcraft

Skill	Description	Purpose
Fire-Making	Starting fires using methods like friction or flint and steel	Provides warmth, cooking, and signaling
Shelter Construction	Building shelters with natural materials for protection	Provides shelter from elements
Knot-Tying & Lashing	Tying strong knots to secure shelters, tools, or gear	Ensures stability and safety of equipment
Signaling & Navigation	Using signals and maps to communicate and find directions	Aid in communication and navigation
Camouflage & Evasion	Blending into surroundings and avoiding detection in wilderness settings	Concealment and stealth in survival situations

Homesteading Projects

Homesteading	Description	Purpose
Installing renewable energy systems	Setting up solar panels or wind turbines to generate sustainable energy	Provide renewable power for off-grid living
Tending livestock or bees	Raising animals like livestock or bees for food and other resources	Obtain food and materials from home-raised animals
Constructing root cellars or smokehouses	Building underground storage or smokehouses for preserving food	Extend the shelf life of perishable food
Mastering outdoor	Cooking meals outdoors using fire	Prepare meals without

Chapter 2
Assemble Your Emergency Supply Kit

cooking techniques	or alternative methods	relying on modern appliances
Making your tools, weapons & gear	Crafting essential items like knives, bows, or shelters needed for survival situations	Ensure self-sufficiency and resourcefulness.

Emergency Kits for Various Crisis Scenarios

These scenarios demonstrate how preppers use smart thinking, physical strength, and mental toughness to survive tough challenges that seem impossible to beat:

House Fire

Imagine you wake up in the middle of the night. You smell smoke and hear a loud crackling sound. Your house is on fire! This is dangerous. The smoke could make it hard to breathe. The flames could burn you badly.

Every home needs an emergency supplies kit with special items just for fires. It should have safety masks to put over your mouth and nose so you can breathe clean air. And long pants and shirts are made of fabrics that don't catch fire easily. This protects your skin.

The kit also needs bright flashlights and headlamps so you can see through thick smoke to find the exit quickly. These supplies let you leave the burning house quickly before getting hurt or trapped.

Once outside, there should be a preplanned meeting spot for your whole family to gather. That way, you can ensure everyone escaped safely and accounted for.

Power Outage

Storms or equipment failures sometimes cause the electricity to shut off in your neighborhood. This means you will not have light, a heating system and AC, or a refrigerator for cooling food, but there will also be no cooking appliances available!

Don't stress; the important things are taken care of in your emergency kit. It contains food that will last long enough to keep you from starving and enough drinking water. It has some thick clothes as well as thermal blankets inside for warmth.

You will see other ways of lighting because they exist, such as candles or lamps, which can be powered by batteries and stored safely; matches and lighters are available for use in starting fires without much trouble. As such, you can keep warm, heat soup, or roast when hungry.

Emergency Kits for Various Crisis Scenarios
The Ultimate Prepper's Survival Bible

In addition, your dependable pack could contain communication devices like a hand-cranked radio or a solar-powered one. With these basic supplies on standby, you would comfortably go through an extended blackout period spanning several days at home!

Injury Emergency

Oh no! You suspect you might have broken your leg while slipping on the wet ground in your dash out. Now you're in big trouble - unable to walk and all alone out here with no one around to help.

Fortunately, you are carrying your compact personal emergency kit, which contains a small first-aid pouch packed with important items.

With these materials and bandages, it would be possible for you to fashion support for your injured limb so as not to make matters worse before seeing a doctor. The analgesics enable you to remain composed and rational while expecting early help.

There's also a loud safety whistle you can blow with your mouth to alert anyone nearby that you need assistance. In addition, the kit has a little compass and map which will show where exactly you are in case you need to phone for emergency services."

Because of this presence of mind regarding such elementary healthcare and sustenance commodities, you escaped what could have been a very dangerous situation indeed: having to grapple with a broken leg all by yourself somewhere deep in the woods! It's always important to have the right equipment!

It is crucial to possess appropriate emergency resources. These go a long way in ensuring that your loved ones are safe and well taken care of during such eventualities. Don't procrastinate until it gets too late. Start now creating an emergency pack

This should include food, water, first aid supplies, tools, and other survival necessities. Before an actual emergency occurs, practice using the supplies that have been gathered. Doing this will assist you in learning how best they should be deployed when the time comes around again. Besides, cooperate with other members within which ye may serve each other

so shall any enemy find himself at great disadvantage. Being ready enables one to overcome tough times like these. With a kit set aside for emergencies alone, nothing unforeseen can scare you.

Your well-stocked supply kit is a great start, but it's only a temporary solution if you don't know how to make your food last. That's where the old-school methods of canning, drying, smoking, and more come in. This chapter is your ticket to preserving food like a pro, ensuring you never run out of sustenance, no matter how long the crisis lasts.

CHAPTER 3
MASTERING FOOD PRESERVATION

It is of great importance to have sufficient food during emergency preparations. Storing foods that don't go bad easily is smart. But you can also preserve fresh foods to have yummy foods ready when needed. This chapter teaches the basics of canning and other awesome food preservation methods.

Food Canning at Home

Canning is a great way to keep foods fresh for a very long time. You need some jars and supplies. Here are the simple steps:

Step	Description	Tips	Things You Need
Prepare the food	Wash fruits and veggies thoroughly under clean water. Peel, slice, or chop into bite-size pieces as desired.	Ensure all produce is clean and cut to the desired size.	Fruits and vegetables, knife, cutting board
Pack the food into jars.	Fill clean canning jars with prepared food following specific canning recipes. Add water, chicken broth, or fruit juice to cover, leaving 1-inch headspace.	Ensure jars are filled evenly and not overfilled.	Canning jars, lids, ring bands
Seal the jars	Place flat lids on jars and secure them with ring bands, twisting them firmly but not too tight.	Avoid over-tightening to allow for proper sealing during the canning process.	Jar lifter, large pot with a rack
Process the jars in boiling water.	Place sealed jars in a large pot with a rack at the bottom. Cover jars with	Use a timer to ensure jars are processed for the correct amount of time	Timer, stove

Chapter 3
Mastering Food Preservation

	water and bring to a boil.	based on the food inside.	
Remove and cool the jars.	After processing, carefully remove hot jars using jar lifters. Place on a towel to cool for at least 12 hours.	Ensure jars are left undisturbed to allow for proper sealing.	Towel

That's it! Canned goods can last for years and years when done properly. Always check that vacuum-sealed jar lids have not popped up before eating the contents.

Shelf Life of Canned Foods

Most canned veggies and fruits will retain their quality for 2-5 years when properly canned and stored in a cool, dark spot. Other canned goods like:

Type of Food	Shelf Life	Storage Recommendation
Soups/stews	2-3 years	Store in a cool, dry place
Canned meat/seafood	2-5 years	Keep in a cool, dark area
Home-canned salsas/sauces	1 year	Store in a cool environment
Home-canned pickles/relish	1 year	Keep in a cool, dry place

Discard any cans that are dented, leaking, rusting, or with bulging lids. Toss out anything that smells or looks spoiled upon opening to be safe.

To make canned goods last as long as possible, keep them between 50-70°F and out of direct light. Avoid temperatures over 90°F.

Methods of Food Preservation

Canning isn't the only smart way to make fresh foods last much longer! There are many other preservation methods to try. Here are some:

Dehydrating

The oldest form of food preservation, dehydrating removes almost all food moisture. This stops microbes from growing and halts enzyme action that causes decay.

Methods of Food Preservation
The Ultimate Prepper's Survival Bible

Dehydrate fruits, veggies, meats, herbs, and more using a dehydrator or oven. Dried foods are lightweight, compact, and shelf-stable for six months to a year.

Root Cellaring

Over winter, this traditional method stores root veggies like potatoes, carrots, and onions in an underground pit or basement-like space.

The cool, humid conditions below ground allow the veggies to keep for months without refrigeration.

Freezing

Freezing halts nearly all enzyme and microbial growth by making foods super cold. Frozen fruits, veggies, and meats taste fresh when thawed and cooked.

But you need a big freezer with lots of extra space, and you don't want foods to melt until they are ready to eat.

Best Ways of Curing and Smoking

These are older techniques to cure and smoke-dry fish and meats for excellent long-term preservation. Salt, vinegar, and wood smoke act to dehydrate and block bacteria growth.

Pickling

Submerging foods in a very salty or vinegar brine keeps them crisp and tangy while preserving them for months. Produce like cucumbers, cabbage, beets, and chiles make amazing pickles.

Sugar preserving

Simple techniques like making jams and fruit preserves have been used forever to lock in flavors, while sugar is a natural preservative.

Dehydrate Foods for Long-Term Storage

Do you like raisins, jerky, or dried fruit? Those are all dehydrated foods. Dehydrating means removing most of the water from foods. This helps the food stay good for a very, very long time!

Dehydrating foods is a super old way to preserve them. People have dried foods in the sun for thousands of years. Drying makes the foods lighter and smaller. It also stops germs and mold from growing. That's why dehydrated foods last so much longer than fresh foods.

Having lots of dehydrated foods is very helpful for emergencies. They take up way less space than cans or jars. And you don't need a fridge or freezer. Just pack them in sealed containers or

Chapter 3
Mastering Food Preservation

bags. Dried foods are also lightweight and easy to carry if you need to leave quickly.

So, learning to dehydrate foods is an awesome skill! You can stock up on long-lasting fruits, veggies, meats and more. Then you'll have plenty of food ready in an emergency where fresh foods are hard to get.

Three Benefits of Dehydrating

Dehydrating foods has so many great benefits:

Space-Saving

Fresh fruits and veggies contain a ton of water weight. But dehydration removes most of that heavy water. This makes the dried food so much lighter and smaller! For example:

Fresh Food	Dried Equivalent	Conversion Ratio
Apples	5 ounces dried	1 pound = 5 ounces dried
Carrots	3 ounces dried	1 pound = 3 ounces dried
Beef	4 ounces jerky	1 pound = 4 ounces jerky

See how dehydrating shrinks the amount of space needed? You can pack way more dried foods into a small area than fresh. Great for small kitchens or storage spots!

Extended Shelf Life

Bacteria, yeasts, and molds all need water to grow. Dehydrating removes so much moisture that it becomes tough for spoilage germs to survive. This extends the shelf life tremendously. While fresh fruits and veggies may last just days, dehydrated ones can keep for five years or more when packaged properly!

Here are typical shelf lives for dehydrated goods:

Type of Food	Shelf Life	Storage Recommendation
Dried fruits	Six months - 1 year	Store in airtight containers
Dried veggies	Six months - 1 year	Keep in airtight containers

Methods of Food Preservation
The Ultimate Prepper's Survival Bible

Dried herbs and seasonings	Six months - 1 year	Store in a cool, dry place
Jerky and dried meat	1-2 weeks at room temp, six months refrigerated	Keep in airtight packaging or refrigerate

Lightweight for Emergencies

Have you ever tried carrying a bunch of big cans and jars? They get cumbersome fast! However, dehydrated foods are lightweight and portable. This makes them ideal for packing in an emergency go-bag or keeping in your vehicle.

Type of Food	Weight Consideration	Emergency Suitability
Canned Vegetables	Heavier, around 15 pounds for 12 cans	Bulkier and heavier to transport
Dehydrated Vegetables	Lighter, 3-4 pounds for a big bucket	Lightweight and easy to carry

For example, a case of 12 cans of vegetables weighs around 15 pounds. But a big bucket of dehydrated veggie equivalents might be only 3-4 pounds! So, dried foods are a great option in an emergency where you must grab food and run.

Two Steps to Dehydrate Food

Ready to start dehydrating your foods? It's pretty easy once you get the hang of it. Just follow these basic steps:

Step 1: Select Appropriate Foods

Some foods work better than others for dehydration. The best candidates are:

Category	Examples	Storage Recommendation
Fruits	Apples, bananas, cherries, pineapple	Store in a cool, dry place
Veggies	Carrots, tomatoes, greens,	Keep in a cool, dark, and dry place

Chapter 3
Mastering Food Preservation

	potatoes	
Lean meats	Beef, turkey, fish	Refrigerate or freeze for a longer shelf life
Fresh herbs	Parsley, oregano, basil	Store in airtight containers in the refrigerator

Try to use very fresh produce at peak ripeness. Avoid overly juicy fruits or veggies that will be hard to dry thoroughly.

Step 2: Prepare Foods

Always rinse and clean foods well under cool water before dehydrating. For fruits and veggies, slice or cut into 1/4 to 1/2 inch pieces. This helps them dehydrate faster. For meats, cut into 1/4-inch thick strips or chunks before dehydrating.

Fruits like apples and bananas may start turning brown when exposed to air. To prevent this, soak them briefly in 1 part lemon juice solution to 8 parts water before drying.

Two Dehydration Methods

There are two ways to dehydrate foods at home:

Method 1: Using An Electric Dehydrator

This is the fastest and easiest way. Dehydrators have stacked trays with fans and heating elements to constantly blow warm, dry air over the foods.

Method 2: Using Your Oven

Place food pieces on baking sheets lined with parchment paper for oven drying. Leave the oven door cracked open a few inches to let moisture escape. Set temp to 135°F and rotate trays periodically.

Drying typically takes 6-36 hours, depending on the method and food. Fruits and veggies should end up leathery or crisp, while jerky should reach a tough, bendable state when done.

Fermentation Techniques for Food Preservation

Have you ever eaten yogurt, pickles, or sourdough bread? Those yummy foods are all made using fermentation! Fermentation is a really old way to preserve foods and make them last much longer. Fermentation happens when helpful microorganisms like bacteria or yeast feed on the sugars and starches in foods. This special micro-snacking causes the foods to pickle and sour slowly over time.

Fermentation Techniques for Food Preservation
The Ultimate Prepper's Survival Bible

But fermenting isn't just about getting foods to taste tangy! It's also an amazing way to keep perishable foods from spoiling for months without refrigeration or canning.

Fermented foods can sit on shelves for ages while keeping many vitamins, minerals, and healthy probiotics inside. That makes learning fermentation skills super helpful for stockpiling long-lasting foods at home.

Benefits of Fermentation

There are lots of awesome benefits to fermenting foods at home:

<u>Benefit 1: Preservation Without Refrigeration</u>

The biggest perk of fermentation is allowing you to keep fresh fruits and veggies safe to eat for a very long time - with no fridge or freezer needed! Most fermented foods are shelf-stable at room temperature, too.

For example, while plain cabbage may wilt and rot within weeks, fermented sauerkraut can keep for 6-12 months in a sealed jar. Fermented pickles, sauces, and condiments have similarly long-lasting shelf lives.

<u>Benefit 2: Full of Probiotics</u>

As foods ferment, billions of healthy probiotic bacteria build up inside. Probiotics are awesome gut-friendly microbes that support digestive health for humans and animals.

Eating probiotic-rich fermented foods helps supply our bodies with these essential beneficial bacteria strains. They assist in processing nutrients from food and preventing sickness.

Most fermented foods are rich in probiotics like Lactobacillus, the good guys that help us feel happy and healthy!

<u>Benefit 3: Low-Cost Food Preservation</u>

Another great thing about fermenting is how affordable it is compared to other food preservation methods. You need basic salt, spices, jars, and fresh ingredients.

With inexpensive veggies in season, you can ferment huge batches of nutritious probiotic-packed foods for pantry storage. Way cheaper than buying pricey probiotics or supplements!

<u>Benefit 4: No Fancy Equipment Required</u>

Fermentation is also awesome because it requires no special canning equipment or expensive gadgets. You're all set if you have a ceramic crock, glass jar, or food-safe bucket!

Fermenting procedures are simpler than complicated water bath canning or vacuum sealing. Just

Chapter 3
Mastering Food Preservation

mix up some brine and let the microbes work their magic.

Fermentation Methods

There are countless fermented foods from all around the world. But some of the most famous, delicious, and easy ones to try at home include:

Method 1: Sauerkraut

It is easy to make sauerkraut as it requires two ingredients only; green cabbage and salt. Begin by thinly slicing a leaf of newly harvested cabbage.

Then, squeeze the cabbage well, kneading with some light salt for a few minutes to remove most of its moisture and begin fermentation.

When the cabbage becomes juicy enough, put it in a clean glass jar or ceramic pot, squeezing it tightly inside. Use your fists to compact the shreds and create a brine.

Finally, use a weight to keep the sauerkraut submerged under the brine liquid as it forms. Seal with a lid and allow 4-6 weeks to ferment at room temperature. The fun sour kraut smell means it's working!

Properly fermented sauerkraut will keep for 6-12 months unopened. Such an affordable, tasty way to preserve cabbage! It's loaded with beneficial probiotics, too.

Method 2: Kimchi

Another beloved fermented food is Korean-style kimchi. This crazy flavorful cousin of sauerkraut is made from salted Chinese or Napa cabbage.

The key ingredients are cabbage, radishes or carrots, scallions, ginger, garlic, chili peppers, and a seasoning mix of salt, sugar, and spices like gochujang chili flakes.

The veggies get salted first to release their juices. Then, you mix in the seasoning paste to coat everything. Pack the spiced veggie mix into a sealed jar.

Kimchi only takes about 1-2 weeks to ferment at room temperature. Eat it fresh or ferment longer for even more funky sourness! Properly fermented kimchi keeps for around six months.

Method 3: Fermented Pickles

Simple cucumber pickles might be one of home's most fun (and crunchiest!) fermented snacks. You need fresh Kirby or Persian cucumbers, salt, spices, and brine.

Start by washing and trimming the cucumber spears. Pack them upright in a jar or crock with garlic cloves, dill sprigs, and peppercorns.

Next, dissolve around six tablespoons of salt per gallon of water to create the brine. Pour this salt water over the packed cucumbers until fully submerged.

Use a weight to keep everything below the brine surface. Then cover and ferment for 4-6 weeks at room temp!

Once perfectly pickled, these tangy fermented spears stay crisp and crunchy for many months when refrigerated!

Practice Your Canning & Preserving Skills

The best way to get good at canning and preserving foods is to practice, practice, practice! Pick up extra cheap produce when it's in season and abundant.

Then, set aside some time each week to create batches of tasty recipes. The more you can and preserve at home, the better skilled and confident you'll become.

Also, remember to rotate through your canned and preserved food supply over time. Eat the oldest stuff first while it's still good. Then, replace what you eat with newly preserved items.

With regular practice and rotation, you'll always have delicious, preserved foods ready. And your skills will be sharp if you ever really need them in an emergency.

Homegrown Food and Gardening

While stored food only lasts so long, eventual resupply becomes critical. This makes integrating renewable home food production into preparedness plans essential.

Converting lawn space into highly productive gardens helps grow nutrient-dense fruits and vegetables, establish fruit trees, bushes, and vines, plant herbs for flavoring and natural medicine, cultivate grains, legumes, and other crops, and store seeds for future growing seasons.

Mastering methods like composting, vermiculture, hydroponics, greenhouses, and permaculture expands capabilities. Composting involves recycling organic waste into nutrient-rich soil. Vermiculture uses worms to decompose organic material. Hydroponics grows plants without soil, using nutrient-rich water instead. Greenhouses provide controlled environments for growing plants year-round. Permaculture designs sustainable and self-sufficient agricultural ecosystems.

Preppers often install rainwater collection systems to gather and store rainwater and use greywater recycling to reuse water from sinks, showers, and washing machines.

For protein, many stock up on preppers canning and preserving goods initially but transition to producing their own via raising chickens for eggs and meat, aquaponics systems with fish and

Chapter 3
Mastering Food Preservation

plants, beekeeping for honey, and small animals like rabbits or goats.

The goal is self-sufficiency and living off the land through an integrated, sustainable, closed-loop food ecosystem covering all dietary needs perpetually on-site.

Hunting, Foraging, and Trapping

In an actual prolonged survival scenario, food supplies will eventually dwindle. This is where developing skills surrounding living off the land becomes critical.

Experienced preppers learn practices like hunting wild game through ethical and responsible methods, safely foraging for wild edible plants, nuts, berries, etc., constructing traps and snares for capturing animals, processing meat and preserving through smoking or salting, and cooking over open campfires and improvising field kitchens.

They have reference guides carefully identifying local edible versus poisonous species. Preppers also know important lessons like following game trails, concealing human scent, and respecting land reserves.

Though it cannot be relied upon as the main source of sustenance, these ancestral "hunter-gatherer" skills are very important since, in difficult times, people may lack food supplies. This is a policy of insuring oneself from dying because of hunger.

By preparing properly in each of these sectors, your loved ones will remain strong and healthy regardless of the state of the grocery stores. It is important to have access to food during this time to ensure one's family will not go hungry when things are difficult.

Case Studies and Real-World Examples

Pack away food into properly sealed bags or containers after completely drying it. You can easily use resealable plastic freezer bags for this. Expel any excess air from the bags by squeezing them. Moreover, one may vacuum pack the bags or employ tight-lidded food storage buckets.

Keep dehydrated foods in a dry, cool, dark place, e.g., basement or store room. Do not keep them in places with high moisture, temperatures, or direct sunlight since this will spoil them with time. Ensure you check on the food sometimes and throw away those with molds or unusual smells.

If you dehydrate and store correctly, you can enjoy eating these types of food for many months or even years! As a rule, remember to consume your oldest provisions first and then replenish them with fresh ones. Here are the casestudies about people who have depended on dehydrated food.

Practice Your Canning & Preserving Skills
The Ultimate Prepper's Survival Bible

Lewis and Clark Expedition

The two explorers, Meriwether Lewis and William Clark, set out on a great mission in 1804. They were accompanied by men they led from the East Coast to the West across the heartlands of America. The objective was charting the freshly bought Louisiana Territory while seeking passage toward the Pacific Ocean.

Before leaving on their journey, Lewis and Clark knew that they had to prepare for traveling for months through the vast, unknown wilderness without many chances for fresh food supply. For this reason, they amassed an enormous quantity of provisions, including some packed in a dehydrated state.

They packed lots of dehydrated supplies, such as:

- **Portable Soup** - Dried veggie soup mix that just needed water
- **Pemmican** - A concentrated food made of dried lean meat mixed with fat
- **"Jerk'd" Buffalo Meat** - Buffalo meat dried into jerky strips
- **Corn Meal** - Dried and ground to make bread later

They needed lightweight yet highly nutritious preserved food, considering their boats were packed with foodstuff. But it still wasn't enough to last the whole 2+ year expedition.

Along the way, Lewis and Clark traded supplies and gear for more food from Native American tribes. This included more dried meats, fish, and root vegetables.

Anything that could be dehydrated or smoked helped keep the team fed. Members also hunted deer, elk, and other game to supplement their rations with fresh meat.

By the time the Lewis and Clark team finally reached the Pacific in 1805, some had lost over 1/3 of their body weight from scarce rations at times. But the dehydrated staples allowed them to keep going mile after mile on their journey of discovery.

Their successful trek across America relied heavily on having preserved and lightweight food supplies.

This allowed the group to travel for weeks with minimal resupply before the next leg. Utilizing food dehydration savvy pioneered the way for future explorers, military campaigns, and adventures.

Anne Sullivan

On July 4, 1887, a young woman named Anne Sullivan was enjoying a beach day with her

Chapter 3
Mastering Food Preservation

students in Massachusetts. One of Anne's 8-year-old students was a deaf and blind girl named Helen Keller.

While wading in the ocean's shallow waters, Anne noticed another young boy struggling and falling in the deeper surf nearby.

Without hesitation, Anne rushed into the strong current to reach the drowning child.

Anne grabbed the panicking boy and began trying to swim back to shore with him. But the undertow was powerful, quickly sapping her strength. At one point, Anne had to let go of the boy briefly to avoid both going under.

The boy went limp and unconscious in the waves. But Anne refused to give up. She finally managed to drag his lifeless body to the beach and immediately began applying resuscitation techniques.

Next, Anne rolled the boy over onto his back. She tilted his head back to open his airway. Anne pinched his nose closed and breathed air from her lungs into his mouth. Over and over, she did this.

After a few scary minutes, the boy's chest finally began to move up and down on its own! He started coughing and breathing again. Anne's quick actions had restarted the boy's breathing and heartbeat after drowning.

Thanks to her determination, the young boy survived this terrifying incident. Anne later said she just did "what her instincts told her" to try reviving him on that beach.

While not a perfect technique, Anne's forceful pushes and breaths essentially provided the boy with life-saving CPR. If she hadn't acted so quickly, he almost certainly would have died that day.

This brave story demonstrates how critical it is for people to learn proper CPR. This knowledge can mean the difference between life and death in an emergency.

The most important things are calling 911 quickly and then pushing hard and fast in the center of the chest without stopping until help takes over.

Haiti Earthquake

On January 12, 2010, an enormous 7.0 magnitude earthquake struck the Caribbean nation of Haiti. It was a catastrophic disaster that destroyed countless buildings and homes in the capital city of Port-au-Prince.

Over 300,000 people were injured in the terrible quake. An estimated 100,000 to 316,000 men, women, and children lost their lives beneath the tonnes of rubble and debris.

But the death toll could have been even worse if not for preparedness measures taken ahead of time by relief organizations.

Groups like the Red Cross had been pre-positioning emergency supplies in Haiti. This included stockpiles of:

- Water purification tablets and portable water tanks
- Food rations and nutrition bars
- Tents, tarps, and blankets
- Medical supplies and first aid kits

Within 24 hours, these crucial survival items were already being distributed in Haiti to those left homeless and wounded by the quake.

Having supplies ready to go right away was a huge help. It allowed the hurt people to get emergency care fast. And everyone had water and basic food while waiting to be rescued from the wreckage.

More and bigger shipments of aid supplies came to Haiti over the next few days and weeks. But those very first pre-positioned supplies were life-savers in those critical first hours after the disaster.

This showed the importance of preparing emergency kits and supplies before something bad happens. You can't wait until it's too late! Being ready ahead of time helps keep people safer.

Preparing at home Like big aid groups, you can also prepare emergency kits. Then, if any crisis hits, your family will have supplies on hand while waiting for help.

A basic emergency kit should include:

- At least three days of water bottles (1 gallon per person per day)
- Easy, ready-to-eat food like energy bars or canned goods with a can opener
- Battery-powered radios and flashlights with extra batteries
- First aid kit with bandages, antiseptic, medicines, etc.
- Blankets, rain ponchos, or plastic tarps
- Basic tools like a wrench to turn off utilities

Chapter 3
Mastering Food Preservation

- Copies of important documents like IDs and insurance cards
- Cash in small bills

Store your kit supplies together in a sturdy tub or bag that's easy to grab if you must evacuate quickly. Check on it every six months to rotate out expired foods and replace batteries.

With some preparation, you can ensure your household has crucial emergency provisions like the big aid groups! Being that ready could end up saving your life someday.

The Great Mississippi Flood

1927, a massive flood put a huge part of the southern United States underwater for months. Constant heavy rainfall had caused the Mississippi River to swell over its banks.

At the time, few people or towns were prepared for such an enormous water overflow. Hundreds of thousands saw their homes and communities suddenly submerged in deep floodwaters.

The disaster turned into a humanitarian crisis very quickly. Most people had little more than the clothes on their backs as they fled the rising waters. Food supplies ran short, with farms and roads washed away.

But some smarter towns and households had taken precautions against floods. They had piled up spare canned goods, dry foodstuffs such as flour and cornmeal, and other necessary things to ensure they did not run out of anything, just in case.

These were ready families; they had a plan if someone came to save them after weeks. It turned out that they were right all along!

For instance, there was Betty Bone Mayfield, who is renowned for this case. The town where they come from, Melville, Louisiana, did not take the flood threat seriously, but they made sense of it.

In their house, there was no danger coming through for more than eight weeks because when it did, the Mayfields' would be able to escape harm-free. They had hoarded some supplies in their refuge; these included drums of clean water, canned soup, corned beef, lentils, etc., known as pulses or legumes.

However, unlike most people around them who quickly used theirs up, the prepared Mayfield family's stock could still be intact so that they broke and took what was inside there at any time. Because of this preparation on their part, they didn't die like others – three words which refer only to some terrible events – during the much-publicized sad 1927 tragedy.

Home Fermentation Case Studies

Fermenting at home is a cheap and simple method to ensure that your storage is full of probiotics and food, some of which will not go bad. Shall we proceed to an excellent case study from the past?

It revealed how important an added storage pantry with nonperishable foodstuffs is in surviving emergencies and calamities. If the usual channel fails, one might require those standby commodities to survive or avoid dying altogether.

Here, we will see another example to illustrate the point better!

Captain Cook's Crew

In the 1770s, a renowned English mariner, Captain James Cook, went on his great voyage three years long throughout the Pacific Ocean.

Scurvy can be dangerous - it is caused by a lack of vitamin C and is characterized by certain symptoms, such as bleeding. This arises from low quantities of fresh fruits and vegetables that most sea captains availed during these long voyages.

But Captain Cook was prepared. The crew had stocked up the ship with tonnes and tonnes of a fermented vegetable dish known as sauerkraut for the journey of historical importance that they were undertaking!

Cook knew that if he preserved food naturally, it would stay good for a while due to its high vitamin contents. The crew members would never miss their daily dose of the spicy, sour-flavored cabbage since they had many batches stored onboard for it to last long after this trip ended.

While other ships suffered terribly from scurvy – a disease that makes one's gums bleed and become lazy – there was no such case in any of those experienced by men who belonged to Cook's crew. Captain Cook's crews proved the immense value of fermented rations in history.

Fermented foods also work great for go-bags since they need no refrigeration and aren't heavy like cans—tasty, low-maintenance fuel for riding out any crisis.

So stock up! Cheap and easy fermentation skills let you build your homemade food stockpile. Even just a few basics like kraut, pickles, and kimchi mean you have months' worth of provisions.

Mastering food preservation skills has helped many people and communities survive extremely difficult situations throughout history. Here are some real-world examples:

Chapter 3
Mastering Food Preservation

The Donner Party (1846-1847)

Nearly 90 pioneers were undertaking a huge westward journey from Missouri to California. When they became trapped by heavy snow in the Sierra Nevada mountains, their meager food supplies quickly dwindled.

As starvation set in, some resorted to eating the bodies of those who died to survive this horrible ordeal. Many historians believe this tragedy may have been prevented if the Donner Party had been better prepared with adequate preserved food supplies.

WWI & WWII Victory Gardens (1910s-1940s)

During the world wars, when fresh food was in short supply, families across America and Europe were urged to grow fruits and veggies in home "victory gardens."

These homegrown crops would then be canned and preserved to provide affordable food supplies when rationing was tight.

This victory garden movement produced millions of jars and cans that were massively helpful to the overall war effort on the home front.

The Mormon Food Storage Plan Members of the Church of Latter-Day

Saints are taught from a young age to maintain a supply of shelf-stable food storage with canned goods, preserves, and other provisions.

This ensures Mormon families have enough food and supplies set aside in case of emergencies, natural disasters, job losses, or other unexpected events that disrupt normal access to food.

Many in the LDS community credit this long-standing food storage practice for helping countless families through difficult economic times or crises.

The Great Blizzard of 1888

After a severe blizzard cut off deliveries for days, residents of New York City narrowly avoided starvation by breaking into the region's vast preserved food reserves.

Farmers and families had set aside these canned and root-celled fruits, veggies, and staple crops for the winter months.

During the great depression and the economic hardships of the 1930s, many impoverished American families survived off home gardens and preserved harvests when little money was available for food. The government pushed home food production and canning to prevent mass hunger.

Practice Your Canning & Preserving Skills
The Ultimate Prepper's Survival Bible

The Siege of Sarajevo

When Bosnian Serb forces surrounded Sarajevo in 1992, the city's food supplies were almost immediately exhausted.

Residents dug community gardens and stored potatoes, beets, and cabbages through the winter to supplement dwindling rations. Many credited these preserved foods with saving them from malnutrition.

While some associate "prepping" with fringe survivalism, the core idea is sound: Be prepared for emergencies to keep yourself and loved ones safe. This resonates far beyond niche communities, too.

A 2012 survey found that 53% of Americans consider themselves "preparedness minds" who believe in having supplies set aside.

Key resources from mainstream organizations like the Red Cross and CDC promote readiness. The two websites created by the government are known as Ready. The government website and FEMA's Ready Kids are there to provide individuals and families with free emergency planning resources.

Preparing is not only accumulating enough food and commodities for oneself. It is also important to learn how to support others in difficult times.

In this chapter, you learned how ancestors throughout history stayed nourished by preserving harvests using amazing food preparation methods like fermentation and dehydration.

Modern preppers and families can use these sustainable techniques to afford their self-reliant food stockpiles at home. This is because they have healthy foods that are dense in nutrients and can be kept for long without spoiling added into the store makes an important precautionary measure taken against all forms of emergency threats on food security among homestead or family unit members. Keep prepared, keep trained, and stay ready to help.

Okay, so you stocked up and can preserve grub for the long haul. But food will only do you a little good if you got nothing to wash it down! Whether it's purifying from a creek or collecting' rainwater, staying hydrated is just as crucial. This next chapter covers all my tricks for locating', storing, and sanitizing H2O so you never go thirsty.

CHAPTER 4
ENSURING WATER SECURITY

Most experts say you should drink about eight glasses of water each day. But water is not just for drinking. You also need it to wash yourself, cook food, and clean things around your home.

The normal water supplies could stop working whenever there is a big emergency like a hurricane, earthquake, or other disaster. That's why it is smart to be prepared with backup water supplies and ways to make water safe.

Create a Water Storage Plan

Having extra stored water is the first step for water preparedness. Every home should have bottles, jugs, or other containers full of clean water saved up. But how much water should you store?

What Storage Plan Do Experts Recommend?

Most experts recommend storing at least 1 gallon of water per person per day. This is for drinking, basic hygiene like brushing teeth, and minimal food preparation. If you have pets, you must also store extra water for them.

For a family of 4 people, you would want to store at least:

Item	Calculation	Total	Recommendation
Water needed per person per day	4 gallons	4 gallons	Recommended daily intake
Water is needed for four people for one day	4 gallons x 4 people = 16 gallons	16 gallons	Daily requirement
Water is needed for four people for two weeks	16 gallons x 14 days = 224 gallons	224 gallons	Two-week supply recommendation

Having a 2-week supply of bottled water is a good basic preparedness goal. That gives you time to develop a longer-term water solution if normal supplies don't get restored quickly.

For long-term needs, you may want even more water stored up. The more water you have, the better prepared you will be.

Chapter 4
Ensuring Water Security

Where Should You Store All This Water?

The best places are cool, dry areas away from sunlight and heat. Places like:

- Inside closets or cabinets
- Under beds
- In garages or basements

It's smart to have supplies in multiple locations around your home. If one area gets damaged, you will still have backup water elsewhere.

Rotate your water supplies by using the oldest water first and replacing it with newer bottles or containers. Most experts recommend replacing all stored water at least once per year.

Suppose that after a major hurricane, your family has lost access to the normal municipal water supply for over three weeks. Thanks to your preparedness planning, you followed these steps and came through the crisis safely:

Step 1: Water Storage

You accessed your backup water storage of 250 gallons that you had prepared and safely stored in the basement and hall closet.

Step 2: Rotating Drinking Water Supply

For drinking water, you rotated through the oldest gallons first while rationing 1 gallon per person daily.

Step 3: Minimize Using a Hygienic Water

You minimized hygiene water usage by skipping baths, manually flushing toilets using a bucket, and avoiding unnecessary water consumption.

Step 4: Purifying Water

After two weeks, you began treating and purifying rainwater harvested from your roof (see Purification Methods section). This extended your available supply.

Step 5: Restoring Water Service

On day 21, crew teams completed repairs and restored your normal water service. Your preparedness paid off!

How Much Water to Store

Most experts recommend storing at least one gallon of water for each person and pet in your

Create a Water Storage Plan
The Ultimate Prepper's Survival Bible

home daily. This water is meant for drinking, basic hygiene like brushing teeth, and simple cooking.

For example, if four people and two dogs live in your house, you'd want to store at least 6 gallons of water per day. That's 1 gallon for each person and 1 gallon for both dogs.

Building Up Supplies Slowly

84 gallons! That's a lot of water to store! Don't freak out, though; you don't need to buy it all at once.

Step 1: Acknowledge the Water Requirement

Start by acknowledging the need for 84 gallons of water, understanding that it's a substantial amount to store.

Step 2: Manage the Cost and Effort

Avoid feeling overwhelmed by the task; plan to spread out the cost and effort over time.

Step 3: Begin Gradual Purchases

Begin by purchasing a few extra jugs, bottles, or containers each week to build up your water supply gradually.

Step 4: Aim for Initial 3-Day Supply

Initially, aim to have enough water to last for the first three days of an emergency, which is a good starting point.

Step 5: Incremental Increase Monthly

Continue adding more gallon jugs to your reserves every month until you reach your 2-week water storage goal.

Step 6: Consistent Effort

Embrace a slow and steady approach, recognizing that consistent effort will ultimately lead to success in building your water reserve.

Sanitizing Storage Containers

No matter which containers you choose, clean and sanitize them thoroughly before filling them with fresh water.

Step 1: Prepare Bleach Solution

Mix one teaspoon of unscented household bleach per gallon of water.

Chapter 4
Ensuring Water Security

<u>Step 2: Disinfect with Bleach Solution</u>

- Let the bleached water sit for at least 30 minutes to disinfect.
- Rinse fully with fresh water before adding your long-term storage supply to remove any remaining bleach residue and ensure safety.

<u>Step 3: Remove Plastic Odors</u>

- If strong plastic odors persist in cleaned containers, create a baking soda and vinegar solution.
- Add the solution to the containers and let it sit for a day to absorb the odors.
- Rinse out thoroughly with fresh water afterward.

Don't Forget Pet Water Storage

Having water set aside specifically for pets is wise, too! Dogs and cats need about 1 gallon per 100 lbs of body weight daily. Smaller animals require less, while larger livestock need even more.

Pet Type	Quantity	Type of Water Storage	Notes on Pet Water Storage Preparedness
Dogs	2	Large plastic container with an airtight lid	Ensure the container is regularly cleaned and refilled.
Cats	1	Ceramic fountain	Monitor water levels and clean the fountain weekly.
Birds	3	Hanging water dispensers	Ensure dispensers are securely attached and cleaned weekly.
Fish	10	Aquarium with filter	Regularly change water and monitor filter functionality.
Reptiles	2	Shallow bowls	Provide fresh water daily and clean bowls regularly.
Small Mammals	4	Gravity-fed water bottles	Check bottles daily for leaks and refill them as needed.

Store your furry friend's water in an opaque solid plastic container rather than a transparent jug letting in light to keep your furry friend's water fresh. Rotate this supply just as you do your human drinking water reserves.

Start Small If Needed

While it's crucial to go big with backup water storage, even just a few extra gallons tucked away can buy you critical time in a shortage.

So don't get overwhelmed; start small and build up supply steadily monthly.

Perhaps you already inadvertently have a start on an emergency water stockpile! Water stored in large frozen gel packs, old defrosted ice packs, or even leftover ice cubes from your freezer can be melted down for drinking in a true pinch.

Purification Methods for Drinking

Sometimes, after a big emergency, water from rivers, streams, or even your home pipes may be unsafe to drink without treatment. Untreated water could contain germs, chemicals, or other contaminants that could make you sick.

Some methods to purify and make any water safe for drinking include:

Boiling

B boiling water is one of the oldest and most reliable ways to kill harmful germs. Here are the simple steps:

Step 1: Fresh Water Source

Collect water from any fresh source, like a river, lake, or your home's plumbing.

Step 2: Boiling

Bring the water to a full rolling boil over a stovetop, campfire, or other heat source.

Step 3: Rapid Boil

Allow the water to keep boiling rapidly for at least one full minute.

Step 4: Cooling

Allow the boiled water to cool before drinking.

Step 5: Safety Precautions

For extra safety, leave the boiled water in the same container, cover it, and allow it to sit for 15-30 minutes to kill any remaining germs.

Chapter 4
Ensuring Water Security

Make sure only to use food-grade containers when boiling and storing drinking water.

Water Purification Tablets

Special purification tablets can be used as an alternative to ensure water is not contaminated. These small tablets have some chemicals, such as chlorine or iodine, responsible for destroying pathogens.

Put the right amount of tablet into the water in a vessel, depending on how big it is. Allow thirty minutes without taking anything inside the glass for the chemistry to take effect.

Step	Things You Need	Quantity
Step 1: Gather Necessary Supplies	Water purification tablets	Depends on package instructions
Step 2: Prepare Water	• Clean container for water collection • Clean stirring utensil (if required)	1
Step 3: Add Purification Tablets	Water purification tablets	As directed
Step 4: Wait	Timer or watch to track waiting time	1
Step 5: Drink	Clean drinking vessels (cups, bottles, etc.)	As needed

Always store extra purification tablets as part of your preparedness supplies. Look for ones approved by organizations like the EPA or WHO.

Portable Water Filters

A third purification option is a portable water filter for campers, hikers, or emergency preparedness. These filters have microscopic pores and other materials that trap and remove germs and contaminants as water passes through.

Gravity filters, pump filters, and filter straws are some common types. Many can filter hundreds of gallons of water over their lifetime. Be sure to change out the filter cartridge as recommended.

Purification Methods for Drinking
The Ultimate Prepper's Survival Bible

There are a few different filter types:

Filter Type	Description
Pump filters	Pump filters have a hand pump that forces water through the filter.
Gravity filters	Gravity filters use gravity to drip water through the filter into another container slowly.
Bottle filters/Straws	Bottle filters or straws have filters built right into portable bottles or drinking straws.

No matter which purification method you use, it's smart to have multiple backup options if one fails or you run out. It is better to be over-prepared than under-prepared regarding safe drinking water!

Let's assume a crisis water purification scenario. An industrial fire polluted the rivers and municipal water supply with dangerous chemicals. To ensure your family had safe drinking water, you followed these steps:

Step 1: Emergency Water Collection

Collected water from the kitchen and bathroom taps before the contamination spread through the pipes.

Step 2: Water Treatment by Boiling

Treated half of this water by bringing it to a rolling boil for 2 minutes. Let it cool, cover it, and allow it to sit for another 30 minutes.

Step 3: Water Treatment with Purification Tablets

For the other half, you added water purification tablets and waited the recommended 45 minutes for them to take effect.

Step 4: Alternating Water Consumption

You alternated drinking the boiled and chemically treated water for five days until the authorities declared the municipal supply safe again.

Boiling and purification tablets allowed your family to get through the crisis safely. You stored extras of both methods for next time.

Chapter 4
Ensuring Water Security

Let's say a big hurricane caused major flooding in your area. Here's how you could use different purification methods to have safe drinking water:

Before the storm hits:

- Buy water purification tablets
- Get a portable gravity filter
- Stock up on bottled water

During the storm:

- Fill up tubs, sinks, etc., with incoming water in case it gets contaminated later
- Try to boil and cool down 2-3 pots of water before power goes out

After the flooding:

1. Strain out any solid debris from the collected water using a clean cloth
2. Use purification tablets and wait for the recommended 30 minutes before drinking
    - 20 tablets for a 5-gal bucket
    - Eight tablets for a 2-gal pitcher
3. Pour water slowly through the gravity filter into clean pitchers or bottles
4. Any remaining boiled and cooled water is also safe to drink
5. Rotate through all three purified water sources while conserving

With tablets, filters, and the ability to boil water ready, your family stayed hydrated through the hurricane disaster when other water sources became unsafe. Preparedness pays off!

Harvest Rainwater

Even if your normal water supplies get interrupted, there are still many other potential water sources in nature and around your home or neighborhood.

One good option is harvesting and collecting rainwater. This is water that falls from the sky during storms. Here is how to collect it:

1. Use clean plastic bins, garbage cans, or other containers with lids to catch the rainfall.

> 2. Place the containers outdoors in an open area like your yard or driveway during rain.
> 3. Remove any debris that may have blown into the containers.
> 4. Treat or purify the rainwater using boiling or purification tablets before drinking.
> 5. Cover and store the collected rainwater in a cool, dark place.

Be sure containers are clean, and never use water collected from areas exposed to chemicals, oils, or other contaminants.

One fun way to store water is by saving plastic bottles and jugs. When you finish a bottle of juice, soda, or other drink, you can rinse it out and fill it with fresh water instead of recycling it. Ask your parents to help collect these bottles over time.

You can reuse empty 2-liter soda bottles or gallon jugs with milk or juice in them. Just make sure they get cleaned well first before putting water in them. No more spills or sticky hands!

Once you've saved a bunch of bottles, they need to go in a cool, dry place away from bright light or heat. Places like a closet, basement, or underbeds all work great. Don't forget to tell your parents where you've stashed the water bottles!

Having water bottles spread out in different rooms and areas is smart, too. That way, if one section gets damaged or wet in an emergency, you'll still have dry water put away somewhere else.

Utilize Alternative Water Sources

Other potential water sources include:

> - Water heater tanks (drain a few gallons from the bottom to use)
> - Melted ice cubes from freezers or coolers
> - Canned fruit or vegetable juices
> - Swimming pools or hot tubs (purify before drinking)

You can dig holes or trenches to collect fresh groundwater from underground aquifers. Just be careful of contamination risks.

Whenever water is obtained from unorthodox sources, always treat it through boiling, purification, or filtering before consumption. In an emergency involving water, a little care taken in such ways as these might be what separates somebody from danger and harm!

Chapter 4
Ensuring Water Security

Consider a crisis alternative water source scenario: A brutal winter ice storm knocked out your electricity and water service for over two weeks. Thanks to your planning, you were able to stay hydrated by:

Step 1: Collecting Rainwater and Snowmelt

Collecting fresh rainwater and melted snow in sanitized trash cans from early in the storm before it froze over.

Step 2: Draining Water

Draining several gallons of water from the basement water heater tank after it went cold.

Step 3: Treating Pool Water

Treat pool water from your backyard with purification tablets before drinking.

Step 4: Digging for Clean Underground Water

Carefully dig a shallow hole near a creek bed on your property to reach clean underground water seeping up.

Step 5: Boiling and Storing

Boiling and safely storing all this harvested water throughout the 16-day power/water outage until service was restored.

Having multiple backup water sources at your disposal allowed you to stay hydrated and comfortable despite not having normal municipal water services available.

Preparedness Water Checklist

Here is a simple checklist to help guide your water preparedness planning:

Water Storage	Purification	Alternative Sources
2-week supply of bottled water (rotate yearly)	Boiling pots/pans	Rain barrels/containers
Storage containers (new & cleaned)	Water purification tablets	Groundwater (dig holes)
Water storage tips (cool, dark places)	Portable water filters	Water heater tanks
		Swimming pools/hot

Utilize Alternative Water Sources
The Ultimate Prepper's Survival Bible

		tubs

Having supplies from each column gives you multiple backup water options during emergencies. The more prepared you are, the safer your family will be!

Don't be unprepared when that big storm, earthquake, or other crisis inevitably strikes. Water is vital to your survival and cannot be skipped over. Ensure your family stays healthy, hydrated, and safe no matter what by following this thorough guide to water security. Get ready now! Your future self will thank you later.

The most important thing is not putting this off any longer. Having ample, clean, safe drinking water is vital for survival. So take that first simple step today: purchasing a few extra bottles or gallon jugs while grocery shopping.

From there, steadily build up your water reserves one small addition at a time. Get creative with inexpensive storage ideas. And establish a routine for regularly cycling and replenishing these critical supplies.

You got the food and water situations on lockdown after those last chapters. But a safe, secure shelter is the next vital piece of the survival puzzle. Coming up, I'll walk you through every step of finding the perfect discreet hideaway location and building yourself an off-grid bunker that'll stand up to any storm or unwanted company. You'll be livin' large with my insider tricks while others are roughing it.

CHAPTER 5
SHELTER AND SECURITY

It matters a lot to have a home that is safe and secure. Your home is supposed to be like some refuge, which offers protection from harm for all inside it.

However, what would happen if the external environment were hazardous due to disturbing factors such as rain, wildfires, or hostile human beings? During such occasions, one needs the maximum strength of security and shelter in their homes.

Studying all these forms of shelter and safety will help you keep your house safe when the time comes. Let's begin improving your house!

Secure Your Home and Property

Think of your house as an armor that protects and keeps your family isolated from the happenings in the environment. You will enhance their safety if you increase the strength and security features of this "armor."

Below are some effective methods of strengthening and securing the outside part of your house:

Reinforcing Doors and Windows

It is important to have strong exterior doors and windows that cannot break easily. You need a door with a solid wood or metal design that cannot be easily kicked through; the ones made from a very thick and strong piece of timber or incorporating metals are the best option.

In addition, it fits dependable locks and deadbolts, so maybe consider including robust metallic entrance gates for added protection. You can also brace doors shut from the inside using poles or other objects when needed.

For windows, install tough security bars or shatterproof window films to prevent them from being easily smashed or broken through. Getting sturdy storm shutters to cover windows during emergencies is another great idea.

Trimming Trees and Bushes

It's important to keep any trees or bushes around the outside of your home very neatly trimmed and maintained. Overgrown trees with big branches could crash through windows during bad storms.

Also, large bushes near your home give bad guys and potential intruders good hiding spots to lurk and sneak around unseen. Get rid of those hiding places!

Chapter 5
Shelter and Security

Secure Fencing and Gates

Adding a tall privacy fence around your yard creates a very effective outer boundary and barrier for security. The fence stops people from just wandering onto your property uninvited.

Install lockable gates across entrances, driveways, or pathways leading into your home's backyard or sides. This allows you to control exactly who can access your house's surrounding area.

Motion Sensor Lighting

Setting up motion-activated floodlights around the exterior of your home is a fantastic security feature. That way, if any person or animal wanders too close at night, the bright lights will startle and scare them away.

You can even get motion sensor lights integrated with security cameras, too. So not only do the lights quickly illuminate anything suspicious, but cameras can record what's happening as well.

Secure Supply Locations

It's also smart to keep all your backup food, water, medical supplies, and other survival gear locked up securely and hidden from view. Dedicate secure indoor locations like a basement room, storm shelter, or lockable storage containers to keep your vital supplies stashed. Make it difficult for burglars to take away anything that they may need during their invasion by allocating safe places inside, such as a cellar, closet, or boxes with important materials inside only. The more hidden and unreachable these commodities become, the safer they will be.

Home Security System

To be completely safe, you should get a home security system that protects every part of your home. A complete system will have parts like:

- Door and window sensors to detect break-ins
- Motion detectors covering all areas inside and out
- Exterior security cameras
- Loud sounding alarms to scare off intruders
- Optional professional monitoring that automatically contacts police/fire when alarms trip

Technology	Quantity	Tentative Price
Door and window sensors	1 set	$150

Secure Your Home and Property
The Ultimate Prepper's Survival Bible

Motion detectors	1 set	$200
Exterior security cameras	1 unit	$250
Loud sounding alarms	1 unit	$100
Optional professional monitoring	Per month	$30

Let's assume a crisis home security scenario. An extremely dangerous hurricane rapidly approached your neighborhood, threatening destructive winds, flooding, and potential looting afterward.

Step to Secure the Exterior of Your Home in Hurricane Crisis

Thankfully, you had taken these precautions to secure your home's exterior ahead of time:

Step 1: Install Permanent Hurricane Shutters

Before hurricane season begins, protecting your home by installing permanent hurricane shutters over all windows is crucial. This provides an extra layer of defense against strong winds and flying debris.

Step 2: Reinforce Exterior Doors

Ensure the security of your home by reinforcing all exterior doors with extra-strength locks and security doors. This deters potential intruders and strengthens your home's defenses.

Step 3: Trim Overgrown Trees and Bushes

Prevent potential damage during storms by trimming back all overgrown trees and bushes surrounding your property. This reduces the risk of branches breaking off and causing damage to your home or nearby structures.

Step 4: Secure Privacy Fencing

Close and lock any tall privacy fencing surrounding your property to enhance security. This helps prevent unauthorized access to your property and adds layer of protection.

Step 5: Activate Motion Sensor Lighting and Security Cameras

Ensure your home is well-lit and monitored by activating motion sensor lighting and security cameras. This deters potential intruders and provides valuable surveillance footage in case of any incidents.

Chapter 5
Shelter and Security

<u>Step 6: Move Emergency Supplies</u>

In preparation for emergencies, such as hurricanes or other natural disasters, move all emergency supplies into an interior-locked basement shelter. This ensures easy access to essential items while keeping them secure and protected.

Home Security Checklist

Perimeter	Entrances	Visibility	Protection
Fencing	Door reinforcements	Motion sensor lights	Alarm system
Locked gates	Window shutters/films	Exterior cameras	Secure supply storage
Clear bushes	Secure locks/deadbolts	Bright exterior lighting	Hidden/locked shelter

Secure the Outer Layers

Your home's outer layers create the first line of defense against potential threats from the outside. Making these sturdy and secure provides great protection. Let's look at ways to fortify these key outer areas:

The Roof

Having a reliable, well-constructed roof is super important. The roof takes the biggest beating from high winds, hail, fallen branches, and debris during severe storms. Reinforce it by:

Action	Material Used	Frequency & Inspection
Using impact-resistant shingle materials	Impact-resistant shingles	One-time installation
Adding protective weatherizing sealants	Weatherizing sealants	Periodically
Clearing it regularly of leaves/sticks	Hard brush	Regularly
Checking annually for any wear or needed repairs	DIY or a professional visit	Annually

A compromised roof can lead to catastrophic water damage and even collapse during extreme conditions. Don't neglect this crucial outer armor!

Secure Your Home and Property
The Ultimate Prepper's Survival Bible

The Foundation

The structural foundation under your home also needs to be solid and well-maintained. Cracks or deterioration here could cause the entire structure to become unstable and unsafe.

Action	Material/Method Used	Frequency
Inspect the foundation regularly for problem areas	Visual inspection	Regularly
Seal and repair any cracks, chips, or holes immediately	Sealant, repair materials	As needed
Install exterior drain pipes to shuttle water away	Drain pipes	One-time
Add support bracing or underpinning if needed	Support bracing, underpinning	As needed

A strong, watertight foundation ensures your shelter has a reliable base to withstand major impacts, flooding, or seismic shifting during disasters.

The Garage

This space requires special security for homes with an attached garage, too, since it provides direct access inside. Take measures like:

Action	Material/Method Used	Frequency
Installing a high-quality garage door and opener	High-quality materials	One-time
Adding reinforced entry doors into the house	Reinforced doors	One-time
Using high-security lock sets	High-security lock sets	One-time
Putting in shatter-resistant garage windows	Shatter-resistant windows	One-time

It's also smart to avoid leaving the main garage entry open or unattended for extended periods, where people could secretly slip inside while you're not watching.

Chapter 5
Shelter and Security

The Yard

Don't forget about securing the yard area surrounding your house, too! Potential threats could attempt to approach from any angle.

Action	Method Used	Frequency
Consider fencing in the entire property boundary	Fencing installation	One-time
Install motion-activated security lighting.	Motion-activated lighting	One-time
Plant prickly or thorny landscaping around windows/doors	Prickly or thorny landscaping plants	One-time
Remove any objects that could be used for climbing access	Object removal	Periodic

Simple measures like these create additional prevention barriers that deter potential intruders from even trying to get near your shelter.

You better think of a crisis security scenario: After weeks of rising neighborhood crime and multiple nearby home invasions, you took these steps to increase your home's outer security dramatically:

Step 1: Installing a Reinforced Roof

- **Action:** Installed a brand-new roof with impact-resistant shingles.
- **Method:** Used impact-resistant shingle materials.
- **Frequency:** One-time.
- **Inspection:** Annually.

Step 2: Foundation Inspection and Repair

- **Action:** Sealed and repaired any cracks in the existing foundation.
- **Method:** Sealed and repaired foundation cracks, chips, or holes.
- **Frequency:** As needed, but at least annually.
- **Inspection:** Regularly, at least annually.

Secure Your Home and Property
The Ultimate Prepper's Survival Bible

Step 3: Reinforcing Entry Points

- **Action:** Replaced the old garage door and entry points with heavy-duty versions.
- **Method:** Installed a high-quality garage door and opener-reinforced entry doors into the house.
- **Frequency:** One-time.
- **Inspection:** Regularly, especially if signs of wear or damage appear.

Step 4: Perimeter Security

- **Action:** Put up a full privacy fence around the property with locked gates.
- **Method:** Fencing installation with locked gates.
- **Frequency:** One-time.
- **Inspection:** Periodically, especially after severe weather or signs of damage.

Step 5: Enhancing Perimeter Defense

- **Action:** Added motion-sensing floodlights and thorny bushes around the perimeter.
- **Method:** Installed motion-activated security lighting and planted prickly or thorny landscaping.
- **Frequency:** One-time for installation, periodic for maintenance.
- **Inspection:** Periodically, especially after severe weather or signs of damage.

With every outer layer newly fortified from top to bottom, your house was finally secure enough to withstand potential threats and keep your family fully sheltered.

Checklist

Layer 1: Shell	Layer 2: Access	Layer 3: Perimeter	Layer 4: Outer Property
Impact-resistant roof	Security doors	Fencing	Motion lights
Reinforced walls/windows	High-security locks	Locked gates	Prickly landscaping
Storm shelter	Garage/entry protection	Motion lights	Clear debris/hazards
Safe room	Restrict interior	Locked gates	Limit climbing spots

Chapter 5
Shelter and Security

	access		

Think of this checklist as a layered approach to hardening the various rings of defense surrounding your primary shelter area. Prioritize making improvements to each "layer" section one at a time.

Defend Against other Dangers

Of course, securing your home isn't just about protection from human-based threats like intruders and burglars. Preparing that sturdy outer shell also helps reinforce against common hazards posed by Mother Nature herself.

Severe Weather Protection

High winds, torrential rains, hail, and flooding can quickly punch through substandard building materials and expose your home's interior fully. Proper weather-resistant exteriors are a must:

Safety Measure	Installation	Preventive Action
Use impact-rated roofing, siding and window products	Installation of impact-rated materials	Reinforce structural integrity
Install permanent storm shutters over windows/doors.	Permanent fixture installation	Protect windows and doors from storm damage
Have a lightning rod system to dissipate electrical strikes	Installation of lightning rod system	Redirect electrical strikes away from the property
Clear nearby trees/branches that could fall during storms	Tree and branch removal	Minimize potential damage from falling debris

These proactive reinforcements significantly reduce the chances of your shelter tearing apart during extreme weather events. A little investment goes a long way!

Wildfire Safeguards

In fire-prone dry climates, taking precautions to "defensibly space" flammable materials away from your home's exterior is crucial. Try measures like:

Secure Your Home and Property
The Ultimate Prepper's Survival Bible

Safety Measure	Installation/Action	Purpose/Preventive Action
Clearing dead leaves/vegetation from the yard regularly	Regular yard maintenance	Reduce fuel for potential fires
Using non-combustible landscaping materials and surfaces	Selection and installation of non-flammable materials	Minimize fire risk in landscaping
Having an available emergency water source for extinguishing	Preparation and maintenance of emergency water supply	Enable quick response to fires
Installing spark arrestors on chimneys/vents	Installation of spark arrestor devices	Prevent sparks from escaping and igniting nearby areas

Pest Prevention

Even smaller nuisance pests like insects, rodents, or other critters continually seek ways to nest or overwinter inside our shelters. Protect your home by:

Safety Measure	Installation/Action	Purpose/Preventive Action
Sealing any exterior cracks or entry points	Application of sealant or caulking to cracks	Prevent entry of pests and intruders
Installing vent covers and chimney spark arrestors	Fitting covers and spark arrestors to vents and chimneys	Prevent sparks and embers from igniting debris nearby
Storing woodpiles/debris away from outer walls	Relocating woodpiles and debris away from walls	Minimize fuel for potential fires
Using repellent sprays or granules around the perimeter	Application of repellent sprays or granules	Deter pests and wildlife from approaching structures

Chapter 5
Shelter and Security

These relatively easy pest control practices keep your exterior shell free of any unwanted houseguests while helping preserve its integrity.

Constant Maintenance

The basic reality is that no matter how well-built, every home's exterior will inevitably deteriorate from constant exposure to the elements. That's why diligent maintenance routines are a must:

Maintenance Task	Frequency/Action	Purpose/Outcome
Regularly inspect and repair any damages, cracks, or decay	Periodic inspection and repair of structural issues	Prevent deterioration and maintain integrity
Annually re-apply protective weatherizing sealants	Application of sealants on surfaces	Enhance weather resistance and prolong lifespan
Routinely clear out gutters and trim branches away	Regular removal of debris and trimming of branches	Prevent water damage and maintain drainage system
Quickly fix any missing/damaged boards, shingles, or screens	Prompt replacement of damaged components	Maintain structural integrity and prevent leaks

Completing a thorough walk-around of your outer shell and addressing any vulnerabilities immediately helps maximize your shelter's defensive life span.

Shelter Building Strategies

Sometimes, the safest option during emergencies is to stay put and have shelter in your home. Sheltering properly can save your life, whether it's due to severe weather or other hazardous events occurring outside.

Here are some of the key sheltering techniques for various circumstances:

Severe Weather Sheltering

When dangerous storms like hurricanes, tornadoes, or thunderstorms with high winds and lightning rapidly approach, you'll need to quickly access your home's most secure sheltered location.

Shelter Building Strategies
The Ultimate Prepper's Survival Bible

The absolute safest spot is typically underground in a basement or storm cellar without any exterior windows that could get shattered by debris. If you don't have a basement available, locate a small interior room like a closet, bathroom, or under stairs on the lowest level instead.

These inner sheltered spaces put as many walls and layers as possible between you and the outside severe weather threat. They also help prevent injury from falling or wind-blown objects by keeping you confined.

Wherever you plan to shelter, make sure it is stocked ahead of time with essential supplies like:

Emergency Supplies	Description	Purpose/Use
Non-perishable food and water bottles	Food items with long shelf life and potable water	Sustenance during emergencies
A battery-powered radio	Device for receiving emergency alerts and updates	Stay informed about the situation
Flashlights and extra batteries	Portable light sources	Illumination during power outages
Basic first aid kit	Collection of medical supplies and treatments	Address minor injuries and ailments
Thick blankets	Insulating covers for warmth and protection	Maintain body temperature and comfort

Chemical or Radiation Emergencies

Accidental leaks or exposures to hazardous chemical, biological, or radioactive materials are rare occurrences. But if they happen in your vicinity, sheltering in place while "sealing the room" is critical.

This sealing process involves:

Step 1: Secure Entry Points

- Shut all windows and doors leading to the outside.

Step 2: Disable HVAC Systems

- Turn off HVAC systems to prevent the influx of outside air.

Chapter 5
Shelter and Security

<u>Step 3: Seal Openings</u>

- Use pre-cut plastic sheeting and tape to cover cracks or openings, ensuring a tighter seal against external elements.

The goal is to create a completely airtight room with no potential for contaminated outdoor air seeping inside. Choose a small interior room without windows if possible. Safely seal yourself with at least two weeks of food/water/supplies.

Civil Unrest Sheltering

In the unfortunate event of riots, looting, or other civil unrest erupting in your neighborhood or city, your home can serve as a secure shelter - but only if you take proper precautions.

Identify a small interior room in your home, ideally without exterior windows in a basement if available. This will serve as your "safe room" to shelter in place while avoiding any interaction or visibility to rioters outside.

In this safe room, avoid all windows, exterior doors, or walls that could be breached or impacted by violence. Have emergency food, water, medical supplies, and battery-powered communication abilities like radio/TV to monitor events.

Suppose a crisis sheltering scenario: A huge, deadly tornado was headed straight for your neighborhood. With only 10 minutes until it struck, your family quickly:

<u>Step 1: Prepare Supplies</u>

- Grab the pre-packed "tornado kit" of supplies, ensuring you have everything you need for emergencies.

<u>Step 2: Seek Shelter</u>

- Go into the innermost bathroom on the lowest floor of your home. This location offers the most protection from tornadoes.

<u>Step 3: Stay Informed</u>

- Turn on the battery-powered radio to receive weather updates and stay informed about the tornado's progress.

<u>Step 4: Take Shelter</u>

- Hunker in the small room for over an hour, remaining safe until the threat has passed.

<u>Step 5: Assess Safety</u>

The Ultimate Prepper's Survival Bible

- Finally, emerge from the shelter once the radio confirms that the tornado has passed and it is safe to do so.

Sheltering Checklist

Severe Weather	Chemical Event	Civil Unrest
Basement/storm cellar	Air-tight room	Safe room away from windows
Interior closet/bathroom	Seal doors/windows	Stay indoors, lights out
Stock supplies	Turn off the air flow	Monitor news/radio
Listen for alerts	Supplies for 2+ weeks	Only call for direct threats

For any emergency where sheltering at home is safest, remember to access your prepared spot, seal it up if needed, and wait patiently while monitoring updates until the all-clear.

Chapter 5
Shelter and Security

Bonus

Alternative Power and Energy

One of the biggest challenges during any major disaster or long-term crisis is maintaining access to power and energy sources.

With the grid inevitably failing, preppers must have backup systems to provide electricity and heating and cooling capabilities. Historical events like Hurricane Katrina in 2005 and the 2021 Texas power crisis underscore how quickly most become debilitated without electricity.

Renewable Power Generation

At the core of most preppers' alternative energy strategies are renewable systems that can generate a sustainable electricity supply independently of traditional utility infrastructure.

Popular options include:

Solar Power

Installing photovoltaic panels and batteries allows harnessing the sun's rays to produce emissions-free electricity.

The vital components are the solar arrays, inverters, charge controllers, and large-capacity battery banks. Systems can be scaled up for increased energy demands. This provided critical backup power during the 2011 Fukushima nuclear disaster in Japan.

Wind Power

Erecting turbines captures the kinetic energy of wind flow, which then spins generators to produce electricity. It is best for rural areas with steady wind patterns and minimal obstructions. It requires clearing land, installing sturdy towering masts, and maintaining the turbine mechanisms. Wind farms kept spinning and generating power through events like the 2003 Northeast blackout.

Hydroelectric Power

For those located near flowing water sources like rivers or streams, micro-hydroelectric systems use water's mechanical force to spin turbine blades and generate power.

Setting up dams, reservoirs, and piping to control water flow is complex. Still, it provides reliable renewable energy, just as large-scale hydro dams did during the Cambodian Civil War in the 1970s.

Integrating multiple renewable sources, like solar arrays and wind turbines, provides redundancy. Large battery banks store the produced energy for ongoing use as needed.

Backup Generators

While renewable systems are ideal long-term solutions, preppers keep backup generators on hand for interim power needs, as they were crucial for maintaining hospitals running during Hurricane Maria's devastation in Puerto Rico.

Portable gas-powered models are affordable and allow quickly spinning up temporary electricity.

However, fuel storage is required, and gas supplies may be limited, so many supplement generators are needed for larger whole-home propane or natural gas units.

Permanently installed and connected to municipal gas lines, they affordably generate abundant electricity for weeks or even months during outages like the 2011 Virginia earthquake that struck a nuclear plant.

To further extend runtimes, preppers incorporate other fuel sources like wood gasifiers that can burn biomass or even homemade biodiesel from used vegetable oils.

Keeping an assortment of options provides maximum flexibility, similar to how European villages maintained mills during the World Wars.

Heating and Cooling

Having alternative heating and cooling solutions protects families from temperature extremes. Preppers install highly efficient wood stoves or fireplace inserts for heating in safe, adequately ventilated areas.

Stockpiling dense fuel logs and chopping axes ensures ample warmth, recreating methods used for warmth during the Russian famine of 1921.

In warmer climates, the more significant concern is cooling to prevent heat stroke, as was seen in the 1995 Chicago heat wave. Alongside backup generators to run air conditioners, other methods include:

- Passive cooling techniques like insulation, window tinting, and ventilation
- Using basement or underground shelters to escape the heat
- Evaporative coolers, solar attic fans, or ground-coupled heat pumps
- Manual solutions like cold water misters and cooling vests

Chapter 5
Shelter and Security

The key is implementing multiple layers of backup heating and cooling options to maintain safe, livable temperatures in any conditions, even harsh winters like the 1972 Iran blizzard.

Power Storage and Conservation

Equally important as power generation is the practical storage and energy conservation to extend availability during emergencies, similar to how factories carefully rationed power during World War 2.

This includes utilizing deep cycle batteries, power walls, and even recycled electric car batteries.

Smart preppers install power-saving measures, too, like LED lights, energy-efficient appliances, and smart power strips.

Homes get insulated and draft-proofed. Techniques like thermal blocking reflect heat for reduced HVAC needs, emulating centuries-old passive cooling designs.

The goal is to build a comprehensive system that produces sustainable power through renewables and generators while maximizing energy efficiency so precious resources are conserved.

Having lighting, refrigeration, communications, and other basics powered is vital, just as it was for those enduring the 2003 Northeast Blackout.

With robust alternative energy contingencies in place, nothing from winter storms to cyber attacks can disrupt your family's access to the electricity and climate control needed for safe, comfortable living - a lesson learned from the 2021 Texas power crisis.

That crucial capability makes the prepper lifestyle worthwhile, providing self-reliance as our ancestors had before modern conveniences.

Self-Defense Techniques

Of course, the last line of defense for keeping your home and family secure is your ability to protect yourself if absolutely required. While avoiding violence should always be the top goal, basic self-defense knowledge provides an emergency fallback option.

Non-Lethal Self-Defense

For general home security, alarm systems, cameras, and good locks (as we covered earlier) are excellent initial deterrents against potential intruders or attackers. However, hands-on self-defense tools can provide extra prevention, too.

Simple devices like these can briefly stun or disorient an aggressor in an emergency scenario:

Self-Defense Techniques
The Ultimate Prepper's Survival Bible

Security Tools	Description	Purpose
Blinding tactical flashlights or strobing disorientation devices	Emit intense light or strobing effect to disorient attackers	Deter or disorient potential threats
Extremely loud personal security alarms	Produce loud sounds to attract attention and scare off attackers	Alert others and deter attackers
Pepper spray or pepper spray launchers	Dispense pepper spray for self-defense against assailants	Provide non-lethal means of protection

These non-lethal tools are designed to temporarily incapacitate someone just long enough for you to get away and call for help from authorities safely. Use only as an absolute last resort for self-defense.

Self-Defense Skills

Along with non-lethal gear, basic physical self-defense skills are also wise, just in case. Taking a simple self-defense class teaches you crucial things like:

Safety Techniques	Description	Purpose
How to identify and avoid potentially threatening scenarios	Recognize and steer clear of dangerous situations	Prevent or minimize the risk of harm
Using body language and verbal commands to defuse situations	Employ non-violent communication and demeanor to de-escalate conflicts	Calm tense situations and prevent violence
Safe restraint, blocking, and striking techniques	Employ physical techniques to protect oneself or others	Defend against physical threats
Understanding reasonable use of force laws	Familiarize yourself with legal guidelines governing self-defense	Ensure actions taken are lawful and justified

Chapter 5
Shelter and Security

Firearms for Defense

For those interested and properly licensed, legally owning a firearm for home defense purposes can be an option for absolute worst-case scenarios of life-threatening attacks.

However, safely owning firearms requires extensive education on:

Safety and Legal Considerations	Description	Purpose
All relevant weapon laws in your area	Familiarize with local regulations governing weapon possession and use	Ensure compliance with legal requirements
Proper safety, storage, and maintenance procedures	Adhere to safe handling practices and storage guidelines	Minimize the risk of accidents and injuries
Regular hands-on training and competency practice	Engage in frequent training sessions to maintain proficiency and skill	Improve readiness and response capabilities

Introducing a lethal weapon like a gun should always be an absolute last resort if there is truly no other way to preserve your life despite attempting all other options first.

Let's think of a crisis self-defense scenario: Two aggressive strangers approached your home late at night while your family was inside.

To handle the situation safely, you took these actions:

Step 1: Trigger the Home Security Alarm

Quickly activate the loud home security alarm from inside the house.

Step 2: Issue Verbal Warnings

Shout verbal warnings that police will alert the intruders and potentially deter them.

Step 3: Retrieve Pepper Spray

If the situation escalates, retrieve your legal pepper spray as a self-defense option.

Step 4: Take Safe Position

Maintain a safe position behind the reinforced exterior door to protect yourself while monitoring the situation.

Self-Defense Techniques
The Ultimate Prepper's Survival Bible

<u>Step 5: Wait for the Response</u>

Wait for the intruders' reaction. The persistence of alarms can often prompt them to flee, as they did in this case.

By combining security systems with prepared self-defense tools, you effectively deterred and removed the threat without ever needing to confront the aggressors yourself directly.

Self-Defense Checklist

Deter	**Defend**	**Escape**
Alarm system	Pepper spray	Safely exit area
Bright sensor lights	Personal alarms	Avoid escalating
Verbal warnings	Blinding flashlights	Call for help

The smart approach uses security deterrents first to avoid confrontation entirely. But if that fails, non-lethal defense tools provide options to temporarily subdue to evacuate and call for help from authorities safely.

Preventing Confrontations

The greatest way to protect yourself is to not get into a dangerous fight in the first place! You have to be aware of what's around you all the time.

If you don't feel good about a situation or place, leave calmly and quickly before anything dangerous can happen. Don't be brave for no reason – there's no reward.

Trust yourself too often; our instincts tell us something when they aren't. If something does seem strange, though, or if your gut feeling tells you something isn't right, it could mean that you have already noticed something bad that hasn't happened yet.

Awareness	Intuition	Risk Avoidance
Being aware without paranoia	Trusting your intuition reasonably	Avoiding unnecessary risks
Knowing basic preparedness skills	Yet not living in constant fear	Think wisely before taking action

Chapter 5
Shelter and Security

With some common-sense precautions, basic security tools, and the ability to safely defuse or remove yourself from conflicts, you can ensure your home remains the secure sanctuary you need.

Self-Defense Priorities

All these security and self-defense measures aim to keep your family safe and empowered - not afraid.

The priorities are:

> 1. Securing your home's exterior boundary
> 2. Having proper sheltering strategies
> 3. Non-violent self-defense is only an absolute last resort

This doesn't mean you must become an elite security expert. Taking basic steps in each area provides far more protection than being completely unprepared.

So start small by covering easier basics like:

> - Improved door and window locks
> - Identifying a sheltering room
> - Purchasing pepper spray or a blinding flashlight

From that simple foundation, you can continuously enhance your shelter and personal preparedness at a comfortable pace over time. The main thing is developing an environment and personal safety mindset focused on reasonable precautions - not irrational fear or overreaction. Your family's sense of safety and security will steadily grow with steady progress and smart practices.

You're stocked up on supplies and hunkered down in a secure shelter. But what good's that if you or your loved ones get sick or injured? This next chapter is all about staying healthy in any situation. I'm talking natural remedies, basic medical skills, and even birthing babies if it comes to that! Don't worry; I'll walk you through it all step-by-step so you can keep your crew in tip-top shape.

CHAPTER 6
HEALTH AND WELLNESS

As you read this chapter, you'll pick up some important skills for looking after your health and well-being when no doctor or nurse is around to help.

We'll be covering basic first aid for dealing with injuries and illness, how to keep yourself germ-free by maintaining good hygiene and living in clean surroundings, and ways of staying mentally strong to deal with stress healthily.

By becoming good at these aspects of self-care, you'll be well prepared to manage successfully should the going get tough – which it sometimes does. And since good health is one of your most precious possessions . . . get ready to fight for it!

Emergency Life-Saving Skills

Lifesaving techniques such as CPR and first aid should be incorporated into every survival plan because dealing with health crises is crucial to being prepared.

When there are no emergency medical services around, some simple knowledge of first aid can help to survive or die. It could even be fatal to wait for medical staff.

This is the reason why responsible preppers make sure that one person is CPR and trauma-certified. In addition, first aid literature and videos should also be included, among other things, in the library of a person preparing for emergencies.

Some core skills are unblocking air passages, stopping blood flow, giving attention to burn fractures, and identifying stroke or cardiac arrest symptoms. It is important to have a fully equipped first-aid kit nearby containing gauze, plasters, disinfectants, and splints, among other things, to ensure such important care can be given when needed.

Advanced preppers may take intensive trauma medicine courses with training on treating gunshots, establishing airways, using tourniquets, and more. With the proper knowledge and gear, many preventable deaths are avoided.

But first aid is just the start. Smart preppers stockpile prescriptions, over-the-counter meds, medical guides, basic instruments like stethoscopes, and herbal remedies. You want supplies ready to handle anything from minor flu to significant trauma.

The key is proper training, the right gear, and well-practiced skills to handle likely medical situations based on your area's risks.

Chapter 6
Health and Wellness

Preparedness ensures loved ones get the necessary care from minor cuts to life-threatening crises.

Dr. Peter Safar, Father of CPR

Dr. Peter Safar was a smart doctor who helped create the life-saving CPR technique. In the 1950s, few people knew how to help someone who stopped breathing.

One day, Dr. Safar had an idea. He wanted to test a new method for getting air back into the lungs and blood pumping again after the heart stops working.

First, Dr. Safar had volunteers act like they were unconscious and not breathing. Then he tried a special combination of steps on them:

> 1. He tilted their heads back to open the airway.
> 2. He gave them two big breaths by blowing air into their mouths.
> 3. He pushed hard on the middle of their chest over and over to squeeze the heart.

Amazingly, this technique got the volunteers' lungs working and their hearts beating again - even after they had "stopped" for a little while! Dr. Safar discovered a way to restart people's breathing and circulation.

He called this new procedure CPR "cardiopulmonary resuscitation." Cardio means having to do with the heart, and pulmonary means involving the lungs. Resuscitation means reviving someone to bring them back to life.

After testing it more, Dr. Safar worked hard to teach CPR to others. He showed firefighters, nurses, and even regular people how to do those simple steps to save lives during emergencies.

Dr. Safar's amazing work made CPR a standard life-saving skill known worldwide. Millions of people have been rescued from drownings, heart attacks, and other crises by receiving CPR.

All it takes is quickly recognizing when someone needs help breathing or their heart has stopped. Then, using that special head-tilt, breath, and chest compression technique can buy enough time until medical professionals arrive.

Real emergency heroes like Dr. Peter Safar proved how smart preparation and basic skills enable everyday people to take action and save precious lives when it counts.

First Aid Basics for Emergency Situations

Being ready for anything means knowing how to care for injuries and illnesses. First aid is very important when help is not close by. You must know the basics to keep yourself and others safe

First Aid Basics for Emergency Situations
The Ultimate Prepper's Survival Bible

until medical professionals arrive.

First aid is simple steps you can take right away to help someone who is hurt or sick. Learning first aid can save a life. It helps stop bleeding, treat burns, and care for breaks and sprains.

Let's say your friend fell off their bike and can't move their arm. You suspect it may be broken.

Here are the steps to follow:

Step 1: Stay Calm and Assess the Situation

- Keep calm and evaluate the severity of the injury.
- If necessary, call for medical help immediately.

Step 2: Provide Gentle Support

- Carefully support the injured area to prevent further damage.
- Avoid unnecessary movement that could exacerbate the injury.

Step 3: Apply Ice Pack

- Wrap an ice pack in a thin towel.
- Apply the ice pack to the injured area to reduce swelling and alleviate pain.

Step 4: Avoid Unnecessary Movement

- Unless there is an immediate threat, avoid moving the injured arm.
- Movement could worsen the injury or cause additional pain.

Step 5: Comfort and Monitor

- Comfort your friend and reassure them.
- Keep a close eye on their condition until medical help arrives.

Following these basic first-aid steps, you help your friend stay as safe and comfortable as possible.

Important First Aid Supplies:

- Bandages (assorted sizes)
- Antiseptic wipes or spray
- Gauze pads and rolls
- Medical tape
- Scissors

Chapter 6
Health and Wellness

- Thermometer
- Cold packs
- Tweezers
- Blanket
- Gloves

Keep a well-stocked first aid kit at home and on the go. Check expiration dates and restock used items regularly.

First Aid for Cuts and Bleeding	First Aid for Burns	First Aid for Choking
1. Apply pressure with a clean cloth or bandage.	1. Cool the burn under cool running water.	1. Ask, "Are you choking?" if they can't speak.
2. Elevate the injured area above heart level if possible.	2. Apply a sterile bandage.	2. Give back blows and then abdominal thrusts if needed.
3. Seek medical care for deep or heavily bleeding wounds.	3. Seek medical care for severe burns.	3. Call emergency services if the airway remains blocked.

Knowing basic first aid can truly make a difference in an emergency. Stay prepared and stay safe!

Let's discuss a crisis scenario: A major storm has knocked out power and brought down trees and power lines in your neighborhood. Your child was playing outside when a broken electrical wire hit them, causing a severe electrical burn to their arm and hand. What should you do?

Step-by-Step Guide:

Step 1: Call for Help

Call emergency services immediately and explain the situation.

Step 2: Ensure Safety

Carefully remove your child from any downed wires or other electrical hazards if it is safe.

Step 3: Remove Clothing

Remove any clothing, jewelry, or items in contact with the burned area. Do not try to remove anything stuck to the burn.

Step 4: Cool the Burn

First Aid Basics for Emergency Situations
The Ultimate Prepper's Survival Bible

Run cool, clean water over the burn for 3-5 minutes to reduce the burning process.

Step 5: Bandage the Burn

Apply a sterile gauze bandage loosely over the burn area.

Step 6: Elevate

Elevate the burned area above heart level if possible.

Step 7: Monitor for Shock

Monitor for signs of shock such as pale, clammy skin, rapid pulse, etc. Keep your child warm with a blanket.

Step 8: Provide Information

Once help arrives, provide any details about the incident to the medical team.

First Aid Checklist

Item	Quantity	Notes
Sterile Gauze Pads	10-20	For covering wounds
Adhesive Bandages	20-30	Various sizes
Roller Gauze Bandages	3-4	For wrapping/securing
Antiseptic Wipes	10-15	Cleaning minor wounds
Medical Tape	1 roll	For securing bandages
Scissors	1 pair	For cutting bandages
Thermometer	1	Digital or disposable
Cold Packs	2-3	Reusable for swelling
Tweezers	1	For removing splinters
Emergency Blanket	1	Retains body heat

When accidents or injuries happen, knowing proper first aid is crucial. Receiving quick care can

Chapter 6
Health and Wellness

prevent minor issues from becoming serious medical emergencies. Stay prepared by learning a few key first-aid skills.

Treating Burns

Burns require special care to prevent infection and further skin damage. For minor burns from heat, fire, or chemicals:

Step 1: Cool the Burn

- Immediately run cool water over the burn for 3-5 minutes to stop the burning process.

Step 2: Remove Clothing

- Carefully remove any clothing or jewelry from the burned area. Do not try to remove anything sticking to the burn.

Step 3: Apply a Dressing

- Apply a clean compress or dressing over the burn using sterilized gauze or a clean cloth.

Step 4: Secure with Bandage

- Wrap the dressed burn loosely with a roller bandage or medical tape to avoid putting pressure on the burn.

Step 5: Avoid Home Remedies

- Do not put ointments, butter, or other home remedies on the burn.

Step 6: Seek Medical Attention

- Seek medical attention promptly for burns covering an area larger than your hand.

Splinting Broken Bones

If you suspect a broken limb, it must be properly immobilized before moving the person. Splinting will prevent further injury and pain. Improvised splints can be made from rigid household items like:

Category	Items
Stationery	Rulers, crayons, or pens are bundled together.
Kitchen	Wooden spoons or specialty cooking tools

First Aid Basics for Emergency Situations
The Ultimate Prepper's Survival Bible

Reading Materials	Magazines, catalogs, or books
Home Improvement	Pieces of wood trim, molding, or yardsticks

To splint a broken arm or leg:

Step 1: Immobilize the Limb

Do not try to realign the bones. Immobilize the limb in the existing position to prevent further damage.

Step 2: Apply Padding

Paint padding like rolled gauze between the splint and the body part to provide cushioning and support.

Step 3: Secure the Splint

Tie the splint securely using cloth strips, gauze, or shoelaces. Ensure that the splint is snug but not too tight.

Step 4: Check Circulation

Check that the splint is not too tight by exposing fingers or toes to monitor circulation. Ensure there is no numbness or tingling.

Step 5: Apply Ice Pack

Apply an ice pack over the area to reduce swelling, but avoid direct skin contact to prevent frostbite.

Step 6: Seek Medical Care

Seek professional medical care as soon as possible for proper evaluation and treatment of the fracture.

Caring for Head Injuries

Any blow to the head should be treated as a potential concussion or more serious brain injury. Do not take chances. Look for symptoms like:

- Severe headache or dizziness
- Confusion, slurred speech, or loss of consciousness
- Vomiting or severe nausea

Chapter 6
Health and Wellness

> - Pupils of unequal sizes
> - Clear fluid or blood from ears or nose

If any of these signs are present:

> 1. Do not move the person unless required for safety.
> 2. Apply firm pressure to any bleeding areas on the head using a clean cloth.
> 3. If conscious, have them remain still and quiet in a comfortable position.
> 4. Monitor breathing, pulse, and any changes in symptoms while waiting for emergency help.
> 5. If unconscious, turn them on their side to prevent choking on vomit or fluids.

It is important to have first aid skills, which can be crucial, especially during emergencies. Seek education so that you are ready!

Suppose an emergency where first aid knowledge could help save someone's life. Imagine that you go for a long walk far away from any cities. Suddenly, your buddy falls down the hill, heavily hitting by a stone and probably having a leg bone fracture. Cell phones don't work here, and it will take too long before you get back to your parked car, but what can one do in such cases, and how could they take care of the injured person in this situation?

Assisting a Friend with a Leg Injury

Step 1: Assess the Situation

Remain calm and quickly assess their condition. If they are unconscious or show signs of head trauma, avoid moving them unless necessary to prevent further injury.

Step 2: Control Bleeding

Look for any obvious bleeding and apply firm pressure using clean bandages or cloth to stop the bleeding.

Step 3: Check Responsiveness

Check responsiveness by asking questions and observing for confusion or slurred speech to evaluate their level of consciousness.

Step 4: Immobilize the Leg

Immobilize the leg by splinting it in the position you find it using improvised rigid materials like

First Aid Basics for Emergency Situations
The Ultimate Prepper's Survival Bible

branches or hiking poles secured with belts or strips of clothing.

Step 5: Apply Padding

Use extra padding like jackets or spare clothes to prevent the splint from rubbing directly on the skin and causing irritation.

Step 6: Check Circulation

Ensure that the splint is not cutting off circulation by checking that the toes are still warm and have good color.

Step 7: Provide Comfort

Give your friend water or snacks if conscious, and make them as comfortable as possible while waiting for help.

Step 8: Move Toward Safety

Slowly and carefully move back toward your vehicle, stopping frequently to rest and check the injured leg.

Step 9: Call for Help

Once able to call for help, request emergency assistance, and convey your location details accurately.

Step 10: Monitor and Administer Care

Continue monitoring vital signs and administering care until paramedics arrive to take over the situation.

Checklist

Item	Quantity	Purpose	Notes
Gauze Pads	20	Wound dressings	Variety of sizes
Gauze Rolls	4	Bandages	2-inch width
Medical Tape	Two rolls	Secure dressings	Cloth adhesive
Antiseptic Wipes	20	Clean wounds	Individually wrapped
Ace Bandages	2	Wrapping sprains	Self-adhering

Chapter 6
Health and Wellness

Splinting Materials	Assortment	Immobilize fractures	Rigid household items
Instant Cold Packs	4	Reduce swelling	Do not freeze
CPR Mask or Shield	1	Rescue breaths	With one-way valve
Scissors	1 pair	Cutting gauze	Heavy-duty recommended
Tweezers	1	Remove splinters	Sharp pointed tip
Gloves	Four pairs	Protect from blood	Non-latex
Thermometer	1	Check temperature	Digital medical grade
Blankets	2	Prevent shock	Emergency/space blankets

Dental Emergencies

When professional dental care is unavailable, having the right supplies to handle dental issues is important:

Dental Supplies	Description
Dental Kits	Prepackaged with dental picks, mirrors, temporary filling materials, and pain relievers.
Zinc Oxide Paste	It can temporarily fill cavities or secure loose caps/crowns.
Dental Wax	Helps protect exposed nerves and relieve pain from broken teeth.
Oral Anesthetic Gels	Provides topical numbing for toothaches or mouth sores.
Dental Clamps	Helps remove objects stuck between teeth when floss isn't working.

Always seek qualified dental treatment as soon as possible for any major issues.

Obstetrical Care

Being prepared to assist with an emergency childbirth when Healthcare access is limited:

Obstetric Supplies	Description
Obstetrical Kits	Sterile packages containing drapes, umbilical clamps, bulb suction, etc.
Sanitized Scissors	For cutting the umbilical cord after clamping.
Clean Towels/Blankets	To swaddle and keep the newborn warm.
Latex Gloves	Multiple pairs to maintain a sterile field during delivery.
Umbilical Tape	Secures clamped cord stump after cutting.

While not a comprehensive solution, these supplies allow basic needs to be met in an emergency birth situation.

Patient Movement

Safely moving an injured person over any distance using proper spinal precautions:

Rescue Equipment	Description
Rigid Splints	Allow for full-body immobilization onto a backboard or litter.
Patient Drags	Durable harnesses or straps for pulling someone across terrain.
Litters/Stretchers	Portable cots or slings for lifting and carrying patients.
Splint Padding	Protects pressure points and prevents further injuries.

Know procedures for log-rolling onto spine boards and properly securing a patient for transport over rough ground.

Having the right first aid supplies tailored to the specific emergency allows you to provide better care when medical professionals are unavailable.

Let's discuss an emergency scenario: You are part of a wilderness expedition when one member

Chapter 6
Health and Wellness

begins complaining of severe abdominal cramping and nausea. As the pain intensifies, it becomes clear she is experiencing obstructed labor and going into childbirth prematurely. What are the next steps using your first aid kit?

Step-by-Step Guide

Step 1: Prepare the Area

Move the woman to a sheltered, private area and make her comfortable.

Step 2: Set Up

Open an obstetrical kit and sanitize the area using disinfecting wipes or diluted bleach solution.

Step 3: Wear Protective Gear

Put on multiple pairs of latex gloves and lay out all sterile drapes, towels, and umbilical clamps.

Step 4: Monitor Contractions

As contractions increase, ensure the baby is properly presenting head-first.

Step 5: Delivery

Once the head crowns, gently guide it out and quickly suction the mouth/nose with a bulb syringe.

Step 6: Deliver the Baby

When the shoulders deliver, carefully pull the rest of the body downward.

Step 7: Umbilical Cord

Immediately clamp and cut the umbilical cord with sterilized scissors, then firmly massage the uterus.

Step 8: Attend the Newborn

Vigorously towel off and wrap the baby to maintain warmth while checking vital signs.

Step 9: Clean Up

Properly discard all soiled materials and any biological waste in separate biohazard bags.

Step 10: Monitor and Evacuate

Monitor mother and baby closely while arranging for emergency medical evacuation.

First Aid Checklist

Maintain Hygiene and Sanitation Standards
The Ultimate Prepper's Survival Bible

Item	Quantity	Purpose	Notes
Dental Kit	1	Temporary tooth repair	Pre-assembled
Zinc Oxide	1 tube	Fill cavities	Non-stinging formula
Dental Wax	Two boxes	Protective covering	Mint or plain
Oral Anesthetic	1 bottle	Numb oral pain	Max strength benzocaine
Dental Clamps	2	Remove stuck objects	Curved and straight
OB Kit	1	Assist childbirth	All-in-one sterile pack
Umbilical Tape	3	Secure clamped cord	Gentle adhesive
Bulb Syringe	1	Clear airway	Single-use
Disposable Drapes	2	Maintain sterile field	Absorbs fluid
Biohazard Bags	5	Waste disposal	Leak-proof and labeled
Compact Stretcher	1	Patient transport	Lightweight, durable
Rescue Blankets	2	Insulate patient	Retains 90% of body heat
Rigid Splints	Two sets	Full body immobilization	Malleable foam or aluminum

Maintain Hygiene and Sanitation Standards

Keeping clean is always important, but even more so during a crisis. Poor hygiene can lead to illness and infection when you most need to be healthy. Proper sanitation protects you and those around you. Where water is limited, waterless hand sanitizers and sanitary hand wipes should be used frequently. Washing with soap and water is best when possible. Be sure to scrub between fingers and under nails for at least 20 seconds.

Brush teeth twice daily with a soft toothbrush and toothpaste or baking soda if toothpaste is unavailable. Floss once per day if possible. Bad dental hygiene can quickly cause painful tooth and gum problems that are difficult to treat in a crisis.

Chapter 6
Health and Wellness

Bathe or take sponge baths frequently using a washcloth, soap, and warm water. Pay extra attention to the underarms, feet, and groin area. Replace undergarments and socks daily if possible to stay fresh. Females should pack enough feminine hygiene supplies for their cycle plus extras. Wash clothes regularly if you can, and air dry if needed. Consider having a portable hand-crank or solar clothes dryer. Avoiding damp, soiled clothing reduces skin irritation and infection risk.

Maintaining a hygienic living space is also crucial:

- Dispose of all trash, waste, and soiled items properly
- Keep a designated toilet area, restroom, or waste bucket
- Bury human waste if no toilet is available
- Wash dishes thoroughly after use
- Keep food preparation areas sanitized
- Control household pests like flies and rodents

Poor sanitation leads to the spread of disease through contaminated food, water, and living spaces. Taking hygiene seriously is vital when usual utilities are compromised.

Crisis Scenario: A major flood has damaged your home's plumbing, and you have no running water. With limited resources, how can you and your family stay clean and prevent illness?

Step-by-Step Guide:

Step 1: Ration Drinking Water

Ration your stored drinking water for consumption only. Do not use it for bathing.

Step 2: Collect Rainwater

Collect rainwater from clean containers or surfaces for bathing and cleaning.

Step 3: Use Public Facilities

Use bathroom facilities at public buildings like stores or community centers while available.

Step 4: Establish the Latrine Area

Create an outhouse or designated latrine area away from living spaces.

Step 5: Maintain Hygiene

Use anti-bacterial hand wipes or sanitizer generously after using restroom areas.

Maintain Hygiene and Sanitation Standards
The Ultimate Prepper's Survival Bible

Step 6: Take Sponge Baths

Take sponge baths using washcloths, soap, and heated rainwater or bottled water.

Step 7: Change Clothes Regularly

Wear clean, dry undergarments and socks daily. Wash clothes in rainwater when possible.

Step 8: Dental Hygiene

Maintain good dental hygiene using baking soda to brush when toothpaste is gone.

Step 9: Prevent Mold and Pests

Keep all living areas dry and waste-free to discourage mold and pests.

Step 10: Food Safety

Strictly follow food safety measures - cook thoroughly and avoid contact between raw and cooked foods.

Sanitation Checklist:

Item	Quantity	Notes
Hand Sanitizer	2-3 bottles	At least 60% alcohol
Anti-Bacterial Wipes	4-6 packs	For handwashing
Bar Soap	3-4 bars	For bathing
Washcloths	4-6	For sponge baths
Towels	2 per person	Quick-dry recommended
Toilet Paper	1 case+	Essential for sanitation
Feminine Products	3+ month supply	Pads or tampons
Trash Bags	1 box	For waste disposal
Disinfectant	Two bottles	Cleaning and sanitizing

Let's assume another sanitation crisis scenario: An ice storm has caused widespread power outages in your area. Your family is taking shelter in your home, but with no running water or

Chapter 6
Health and Wellness

electricity for the foreseeable future, how can you properly maintain hygiene and sanitation?

Step-by-Step Guide:

1. Set up a makeshift shower area using tarps or sheets for privacy. Heat non-drinking water for bathing.
2. Take frequent sponge baths using warm water, washcloths, and biodegradable soap.
3. Wash hair by wetting first, lathering with a small amount of shampoo, then rinsing thoroughly.
4. Establish a designated outhouse area well away from your shelter and water sources.
5. Use sanitizing solution frequently in the outhouse pit to control germs and odors.
6. Do laundry by plunging clothes in warm, soapy water, then rinsing and wringing thoroughly.
7. Air dry all clothing and linens in an indoor drying area if possible.
8. Use alcohol-based hand sanitizer or sanitizing wipes rigorously after bathroom use and before meals.
9. Keep all living areas dry and waste-free to discourage mold and pests.
10. Filter and treat any collected water before using it for hygiene to kill bacteria.

Sanitation Checklist

Item	Quantity	Purpose	Notes
Solar Shower Bag	2	Bathing water	Heats in sun
Biodegradable Soap	6 bars	Bathing/Dishes	Camp-style
Washcloths	12	Sponge baths	Anti-bacterial
Bath Towels	6	Drying off	Quick-dry
Toilet Seat/Lid	2	Outhouse	With sanitation chemicals
Sanitation Tarp	1	Privacy shelter	For outhouse

Maintain Hygiene and Sanitation Standards
The Ultimate Prepper's Survival Bible

5-Gal Bucket	2	Hand-washing	With tap
Baby Wipes	Eight packs	Freshening up	Fragrance-free
Dry Shampoo	Two bottles	Between washings	Powder or spray
Plunger Stick	1	Laundry agitator	Wood or plastic
Detergent Packs	12	Laundry/Dishes	Biodegradable
Clotheslines	2	Air drying	With clips/pins
Hand Sanitizer	Four bottles	Killing germs	At least 60% alcohol

When normal water and utilities are unavailable, getting creative with hygiene is very important. You must take extra steps to avoid getting sick from germs and bacteria.

By being prepared with first aid knowledge, sanitation supplies, and mental health tools, you can overcome emergencies and difficult periods with resilience and strength. Your health and wellness are the foundation for surviving any crisis. Stay ready, safe, and healthy no matter what comes your way.

One option is setting up a camping shower or bathing area. Use a portable camp shower bag or hang a large jug with a nozzle. Heat non-drinking water over a camp stove or fire pit for bathing. Set up privacy screens with tarps or sheets. Place a plastic liner or tarp with buckets to catch used water on the ground.

If showering is not possible, do sponge baths frequently. Wet a clean cloth or wipe with heated water and wipe down your entire body, including under arms, feet, groin, and face. Be sure to dry thoroughly after using a clean towel. Baby wipes are another quick option for freshening up.

Washing hair doesn't require a lot of water. Wet your hair, lather minimally with a dollop of shampoo, then rinse thoroughly with small amounts of captured water. Let hair air dry if needed. Dry shampoo powder can also be used between washings.

Use a large bucket or tub with a plunger-style agitator stick for laundry. Add water and a small amount of detergent, then plunge clothing items up and down to clean. Rinse by plunging in fresh water and wringing out well. Hang or lay flat to air dry.

Chapter 6
Health and Wellness

Designated bathroom areas must be kept very clean and sanitized. Use a separate toilet tent or portable camp toilet if possible. An outhouse can be dug in the ground and enclosed for privacy. Mix sanitizing solution regularly in the outhouse pit to control odors and germs.

Handwashing is crucial anytime you use bathroom facilities or before preparing food. Use biodegradable camper's soap and capture water for reheating if needed. When water is extremely scarce, use alcohol-based sanitizer or sanitizing wipes.

Being Prepared Can Save Lives

Knowing the right emergency preparedness information and having key supplies ready can save lives during crises.

Here are some crucial skills and safety steps:

CPR and First Aid

Certification in CPR and basic first aid can enable you to provide life-saving care in an emergency until professionals arrive. Properly administered CPR has helped restart countless hearts and prevented brain damage from lack of oxygen.

First aid skills like dressing wounds, treating shock, or handling broken bones are also vital. Regularly renew your certifications and keep well-stocked first aid kits at home, in vehicles, and workplaces.

Emergency Supplies

Every home should have a minimum supply of essential items prepared in case of evacuation or disruption to utilities and services. Recommended supplies include:

- 1 gallon of water per person per day for drinking and sanitation
- At least a 3-day supply of non-perishable foods
- Battery-powered radio and flashlight with extra batteries
- First aid kit and necessary medications
- Sanitation supplies like toilet paper, hygiene items, and garbage bags
- Tools like a wrench to turn off utilities
- Blankets, warm clothes, and sturdy shoes
- Cash, copies of ID/documents, and a full gas tank if evacuating

Being Prepared Can Save Lives
The Ultimate Prepper's Survival Bible

Learning CPR and Rescue Breathing

Quickly receiving CPR (cardiopulmonary resuscitation) from someone nearby can save a life when the heart stops beating or breathing is obstructed. CPR acts to pump oxygen into the blood until emergency responders arrive. Here are the basic steps for children and adults:

1. Check for responsiveness and breathing. Shake or tap the person and ask loudly, "Are you ok?"

2. If there is no response, call 911 immediately. Or have someone else call if others are present.

3. Position the person on their back and kneel beside them. Open the airway by tilting the head back gently.

4. Check for breathing by looking for chest rising/falling and listening near the mouth for 5-10 seconds.

5. If not breathing normally, begin CPR. For adults, place one hand on the other and push hard and fast in the center of the chest, at least 100 pushes per minute. Let the chest rise completely between pushes.

6. After every 30 chest pushes, give rescue breaths by pinching the nose shut, creating a seal over the mouth with your mouth, and giving two short breaths to make the chest rise.

7. Keep alternating 30 chest pushes with two breaths.

For children, use one hand for chest pushes and give gentler puffs for breaths. For infants, use just two fingers for chest pumps and tiny puffs.

Family Emergency Planning

Every family should have an official emergency plan and practice drills regularly. Identify two predetermined meeting places in case you get separated - one nearby and one outside your neighborhood. Assign roles like who will take care of pets.

Keep hard copies of contact info and a map marked with home/school/work evacuation routes. Teach kids how and when to call emergency services like 911.

At School

Schools always organize fire and safety drills to familiarize students with the appropriate ways of handling emergencies, schools These children recognize safe places; there are strategies in place for earthquakes or burglars, they take cover, and evacuation practices are done. Even the

Chapter 6
Health and Wellness

educators and other employees learn what to do during unforeseen circumstances.

Mental and Physical Health

Intelligent preppers understand that to survive, one must have the right supplies and plans, but one must also be tough in mind and body. It all starts with being strong.

To be fit enough for prepping, one must have strength, endurance, agility, and stamina. This might mean carrying heavy loads over long distances or engaging in difficult menial tasks to strengthen security in shelters or fortifying them against intruders and exhausting exercises to obtain primary commodities.

The first thing on the list for preppers is taking care of their health through cardiovascular exercises that help keep fit, followed by body exercise that strengthens immunity. They engage themselves with games and other forms of mobility in open spaces and feed on good food containing balanced diet enriched with essential nutrients.

However, resilience encompasses more than mere physical activity. In addition, preppers practice cross-training in crucial survival skills such as orienteering, emergency house-building, hunting/fishing, and martial arts so that these become intuitive actions on their part when faced with danger or hunger.

This also takes into account mental and emotional fitness. Being calm and collected amidst intense pressure distinguishes survivors of emergencies from panicking individuals. Mental and emotional fitness should not be left out either.

Remaining calm and rational under extraordinarily high-stress conditions separates those who survive crises from those who easily give in to panic. Meditation, breath control techniques, psychotherapy – all serve as additional means to develop an indivisible character resistance.

They plan because they know that people would feel bad even just thinking of something horrible that happened once upon a time, and they may also see it today due to lack of food, etc. The plan accounts for having coping mechanisms to deal with normal human feelings like anxiety, sadness, or loss. Stoic philosophies provide needed perspectives and frameworks.

Physical hardiness should combine effectively with mental acuity. Such a brilliant combination produces courage, enabling people to overcome difficult times with ingenuity and determination.

Taking care of your health and well-being is crucial, especially in emergencies or disasters. The first aid skills you have acquired here can be useful in attending to minor injuries and illnesses.

Simple as they are, these techniques range from stopping blood flow using pressure points down to immobilizing fractures with splints available within arms reach until qualified medical

Being Prepared Can Save Lives
The Ultimate Prepper's Survival Bible

personnel arrive on the scene. To accomplish this goal, keep a fully-equipped first aid kit, which must contain appropriate drugs that can be used during the emergency period.

This section has also covered the importance of hygiene and sanitation measures in averting diseases and infections. When there is little water or no tap, one should solve problems related to washing up, like bathing without any hygienic materials, cleaning floors when necessary, and disposing of wastes properly. Keeping a high level of cleanliness for yourself inside the surrounding environment will ensure maximum safety for all members of the family unit.

At last, during times of emergency, it is important to take care of your mental health the same way you do for the physical part. We took several approaches on how best to deal with stress and panic in a positive manner. Activities such as writing therapy, artwork, inspirational literature reading, and taking time out help to refocus your attention. Above all, keep in touch with those from whom you draw strength.

You've acquired the knowledge to stay healthy, but what if the situation escalates and you need to evacuate? It's not about aimless wandering. In the next section, I'll provide comprehensive backup plans and routes for a strategic evacuation, whether by vehicle or on foot. We'll ensure you're never caught without an exit strategy when the situation becomes critical. My mobility tips will keep you one step ahead, instilling a sense of confidence in your preparedness.

CHAPTER 7
MOBILITY AND EVACUATION PLANS

In calamity, a well-thought-out means of getting out of the house safely and quickly could be crucial.

For one to move away from dangerous places easily in events such as wildfire and flooding, they need some form of mobility or evacuation plan.

This chapter concentrates on formulating escape paths and setting meeting venues to make your movement out and that of your family members orderly and in a unit manner.

If you anticipate well and exercise moving-out procedures, you will have better odds of remaining unharmed in times of crisis.

Create Evacuation Routes And Rally Points

It is advisable to abandon your house in certain cases. One needs to determine the safest escape route that leads them to a predetermined point of destination. Making proper plans and thinking about moving out in advance is crucial because this might help keep you safe and sound.

Evacuation Routes are multiple ways identified at which one can leave, such as the use of the primary means of transport or major roads from their residence, and lead towards different destinations. Make a simple map and keep copies in your vehicle and go-bag.

It's wise to have at least two different routes going opposite directions. One route may become blocked or impassable due to the crisis. Flexibility is assured if you have alternatives.

As you move along, identify certain meeting points or rally points that will serve as temporal resting points before reaching a final safe point. Rally points may be:

- Friends' or relatives' homes
- School or community center
- Church or place of worship
- Park, campground, or open area

Rally points act as checkpoints along your route where your family can reunite if separated. They also provide temporary shelter to re-evaluate plans if conditions change.

Pre-establishing rally points gives you and your household a clear place to navigate during the

Chapter 7
Mobility And Evacuation Plans

chaos of an evacuation. Be sure everyone knows the addresses and basic directions.

If time allows, before evacuating, take basic supplies with you like:

- Water and non-perishable food
- Clothes, shoes, hygiene items
- Medications and first aid kit
- Important documents and cash
- Communication/navigation devices

Above all, don't delay leaving if ordered to evacuate or your safety is at immediate risk. Getting out takes priority over gathering supplies. You can access resources at your rally point.

Planning and practicing your evacuation routes ahead of time significantly increases your chances of getting out safely and reuniting if you are separated from your family. Stay prepared!

Consider a crisis scenario: A rapidly spreading wildfire is closing in on your neighborhood. Emergency officials are ordering mandatory evacuations with only a few hours notice. What steps should you take to quickly and safely evacuate your household?

Step-by-Step Guide

Step 1: Stay Calm and Prepare

Remain calm and immediately retrieve your pre-packed go-bags and emergency supplies.

Step 2: Load Up Your Vehicle

Load your vehicle with bags, emergency supplies, and any extra food and water you've prepared.

Step 3: Secure Your Home

Secure your home by closing all windows and doors. If possible, turn off utilities to prevent hazards.

Step 4: Check Evacuation Route

Check your primary evacuation route for any blockages from smoke or fire.

Step 5: Follow the Primary Route

If the primary route is clear, travel directly towards your closest pre-determined rally point.

Step 6: Use the Secondary Route

Create Evacuation Routes And Rally Points
The Ultimate Prepper's Survival Bible

If the primary route is inaccessible, take your secondary evacuation route to the rally point.

<u>Step 7: Reunite at Rally Point</u>

Once you reach the rally point, reunite with and account for all family members.

<u>Step 8: Assess Conditions</u>

From the rally point, monitor conditions and determine if you need to continue evacuating.

<u>Step 9: Pass-Through Shelters</u>

Pass through temporary shelters if conditions make it unsafe to continue traveling.

<u>Step 10: Remain Vigilant</u>

Remain vigilant and follow official guidance on evacuation orders and routes.

Evacuation Checklist

Item	Quantity	Notes
Printed Maps	2-3 sets	Highlight routes/rally points
Go-Bags	1 per person	Clothes, supplies, documents
Water	1 gal per person	For drinking and sanitation
Non-Perishable Food	Three day supply	Protein bars, dried fruit, etc.
Chargers/Batteries	Variety	For phones, radio, devices
Medications	Two week supply	For all family members
Pet Supplies	As needed	Food, leashes, records
Cash	Small bills	For gas, supplies, lodging

Map Your Area's Resources

Locate potentially life-saving resources within a reasonable walking distance from your home using maps or mapping apps. Mark things like:

Chapter 7
Mobility And Evacuation Plans

Category	Examples	Purpose
Water Sources	Rivers, lakes, streams, reservoirs	Provide hydration
Public Buildings	Schools, libraries, fire stations	Serve as temporary shelters
Medical Facilities	Hospitals, clinics	Access supplies or medical aid
Food Sources	Grocery stores, farms, agricultural co-ops	Provide sustenance
Hiking Trails	Parks, greenways	Serve as evacuation routes away from roads

Get familiar with these resources' locations, distances, and multiple access points from your home. They may become vital waypoints.

Choose Rally Points

While traveling on foot, designate rally points - temporary areas where your group can reunite, rest and assess next steps:

> Parks or Campgrounds with water access and open areas.
>
> Stores that are large with shelter and supply reserves.
>
> Areas for worship or community centers are seen as secure places.
>
> Short breaks in trail shelters or underpasses.

Depending on the probable crisis, certain rally points might serve better as regroup areas than others. Ensure that there are different routes connecting them.

Route Planning Considerations

Factors to consider while mapping pedestrian evacuation routes include:

Create Evacuation Routes And Rally Points
The Ultimate Prepper's Survival Bible

Category	Examples	Purpose
Accessibility	Routes clear of major obstacles	Ensure smooth movement without hindrances
Concealment	Paths avoiding overly exposed areas	Minimize visibility to potential threats
Terrain	Gentler slopes, established trails	Enhance ease of travel and reduce physical exertion
Mileposts	Distances between marked points	Aid in pacing, timing, and navigation

If you have no choice but to walk, stick to specific paths and meeting places to save energy instead of wandering about.

Practice Walking Routes

To evaluate the workability of planned paths, you must follow them physically while noting some alternatives for difficult places such as hills. Try out some loads to increase your stamina and see if they are comfortable.

Leave inconspicuous signs on trails using unique identifiers such as tied clothes or chalk marks placed by yourself only. This will make it easier to follow back on yourself under pressure or in an emergency.

When you think ahead and plan well, there are ways through which you can develop all-inclusive escape strategies.

Imagine a situation where there has been a massive earthquake in your town, and the whole place is blocked up. In this situation, the available personnel cannot offer any help.

Step-by-Step Guide:

1. Collect your ready-packed go-bags with Snergy food bars, water, clothes, medicine, and other important things.
2. Print regional maps highlighting potential walking routes with water sources, shelters, and checkpoints.

Chapter 7
Mobility And Evacuation Plans

3. Pack a lightweight bugout backpack or frame carrier to distribute supplies and gear among your group.

4. Bring rugged footwear, trekking poles, and sun/rain protection to navigate harsh conditions.

5. Prepare self-defense items like pepper spray, a folding blade, and a high-decibel emergency whistle.

6. Compile backup navigation tools like compasses and pre-loaded GPS devices with regional topography.

7. Include ways to start fires, purify water, and administer basic mobile first aid.

8. Carry ID, cash, and other critical documents secured in waterproof protectors.

9. Properly mark your planned starting point, routes, and rally areas on a physical map.

10. Stay alert, move as a unified group, and avoid populated areas orQeFjopen confrontation.

Pedestrian Evacuation Checklist

Item	Quantity	Purpose	Notes
Printed Maps	2-3	Route planning	Highlight checkpoints
Hydration Packs	1 per person	Portable water	Insulated reservoir style
Trekking Poles	1 pair per	Stability/endurance	Adjustable anti-shock
Emergency Bivvy	1 per person	Insulating shelter	Lightweight, waterproof
Solar Charger	2	Device power	Guided for positioning
Firestarters	1 kit	Start campfires	Flint/steel, tinders
First Aid Kit	1	Treat injuries	Trauma pads, medications
Multi-Tool	1 per person	Utility device	Knife, pliers, drivers
Signaling Mirrors	2 per group	Emergency comms	Unbreakable, guided

Compass	1 per person	Ground navigation	Accurate orienteering
Toiletry Kit	1 per person	Hygiene & sanitizing	All-in-one convenience
Water Filters	2-3	Potable hydration	Portable purifiers

Planning multiple escape routes from your home or community is crucial for emergencies. But you must also consider scenarios where getting out on foot becomes necessary. Identify walkable evacuation routes and safe areas to travel towards.

Vehicle Preparedness And Maintenance

Your vehicle can be a vital piece of emergency equipment for evacuating or being mobile during a crisis. It's crucial to keep it well-maintained and properly stocked with supplies.

Perform basic maintenance regularly to ensure reliable vehicle operation:

Task	Description	Purpose
Check all fluid levels.	Oil, coolant, brake, power steering	Ensure proper functioning of vehicle systems.
Inspect tire tread and pressure.	Replace if worn	Maintain safe driving conditions.
Test battery and replace if needed	Ensure reliable starting and electrical systems	Prevent breakdowns due to battery failure
Check the operation of lights, signals, wipers	Ensure visibility and safety	Maintain proper functioning of vehicle controls

Keep your gas tank at least half full at all times. During an emergency, gas stations may have outages or long lines. Preplanning helps prevent getting stranded without fuel.

Pack an in-vehicle emergency kit stocked with:

- First aid supplies
- Jumper cables

Chapter 7
Mobility And Evacuation Plans

- Basic tools (wrenches, pliers, multi-tool)
- Tow strap and bungee cords
- Fix-A-Flat tire inflator
- Rags and paper towels
- Drinking water and non-perishable snacks
- Blankets or thermal emergency bivvy
- Cash and coins for gas/tolls
- Shovel and bag of sand/salt for traction

It's also wise to keep an extra spare tire properly inflated in your vehicle and a jack and lug wrench for changing it.

For winter conditions, pack a lightweight snowbrush and ice scraper. If stuck on ice or snow, kitty litter or traction mats can help gain traction.

Always inform others of your intended travel route and expected arrival times. Have a contingency plan if problems arise and you must take an alternate route.

With proper preparation, your vehicle can transport you and supplies to safer locations in an emergency.

Crisis Scenario: You must evacuate your home quickly due to an encroaching flood. As you ready your vehicle, you notice a flat front tire. What should you do?

Step-by-Step Guide:

Step 1: Stay Calm and Prepare

Stay calm and assess the situation. Ensure your emergency kit and spare tire/tools are easily accessible.

Step 2: Remove the Flat Tire

Using your vehicle's jack and lug wrench, safely remove the flat tire from the vehicle.

Step 3: Mount the Spare Tire

Mount the fully inflated spare tire securely according to your vehicle's instructions.

Step 4: Load Emergency Supplies

Load your emergency kit, go-bags, and any other supplies you've prepared into the vehicle.

Vehicle Preparedness And Maintenance
The Ultimate Prepper's Survival Bible

Step 5: Check the Spare Tire

Visually inspect and feel the spare tire to ensure it is properly inflated.

Step 6: Drive Carefully

Drive your vehicle at reduced speeds using the spare tire, being cautious of road conditions.

Step 7: Travel to Evacuation Rally Point

Travel directly to your predetermined evacuation rally point using mapped routes.

Step 8: Arrange for Tire Repair

Once safely evacuated, arrange to repair or replace the flat tire as soon as possible.

Step 9: Restock Emergency Supplies

Restock any used emergency kit supplies to ensure you're prepared for future emergencies.

Step 10: Refill Fuel

Refill your vehicle with fuel as soon as possible, conserving fuel as you drive to the next destination.

Vehicle Emergency Checklist

Item	Quantity	Notes
Spare Tire	1	Properly inflated
Lug Wrench	1	Matches the vehicle's lug nuts
Tire Jack	1	Scissor or hydraulic
Fix-a-Flat	1 can	temporarily inflate a flat tire
Jumper Cables	1 set	Rubber-coated, heavy gauge
Road Flares	4	For visibility/warning vehicles
Reflective Triangles	3	For visibility/warning vehicles
Ice Scraper	1	Telescoping

Chapter 7
Mobility And Evacuation Plans

Snow Brush	1	Extendable head
Tarp/Raincoat	1	For working outdoors

Off-Road Capabilities

If you may need to travel over rugged terrain or unimproved roads during a crisis, consider enhancing your vehicle's off-road abilities:

- Install thicker all-terrain or mud-terrain tires with aggressive tread patterns for better traction.
- Add a brush guard or bull bar to the front to protect vital components from debris and impacts.
- For trucks/SUVs, invest in heavy-duty skid plates to shield the undercarriage.
- Equip a truck bed or roof rack to increase storage space for emergency gear.
- Install tow hooks, D-ring mounts, and a winch if your vehicle may need extraction.

Always adjust your driving technique appropriately for any off-road conditions you encounter. Maintain lower speeds, use proper gear ranges, and avoid aggressive maneuvering.

Emergency Fuel Storage

Gas pumps might fail to work during long emergencies, hence the importance of extra fuel reserves. It is important to safely store enough petrol and diesel while observing the right rules for handling and using containers.

- Make sure that you utilize the authorized movable fuel storage tanks and cans.
- Seal containers tightly if not sealed to avoid vapor escape and make them stable enough.
- Add stabilizers meant for inhibiting spoilage in stored fuel alongside other similar preservative chemicals.
- Dispose of and replace any fuel reserves accumulated before one year to keep a new stock of petrol only.
- Place fuels at all times in safe places, separate from homes, with good airflow.

Extreme care should be taken while learning how to draw fuel from other immobile vehicles because it might be needed at certain times when the resources are almost finished.

Electrical System Backups

To prevent being stuck without a way of getting out during an emergency evacuation due to some unforeseen electrical issues such as bad alternator or dead battery, take the following precautions:

- Keep a heavy-duty replaceable battery on hand before yours fails.
- Equip your vehicle with a crank, solar, or portable generator backup power source.
- Hardwire a secondary deep-cycle battery to provide emergency electrical reserves.
- Install a battery isolation switch to preserve charges between main and auxiliary batteries.

Emergency Communications

During an emergency, it would be ideal to have a means of transport that can allow you to establish a movable communication hub so that you can remain updated and in touch with others.

Action	Description	Benefit
Mount a roof or hood-mounted operating antenna.	Install an antenna on the roof or hood of your vehicle to extend the radio range.	It enhances the radio communication range, allowing better contact with your network or emergency services.
Equip CB radios, GMRS/FRS walkie-talkies, and NOAA weather radio receivers	Install communication devices like CB radios, GMRS/FRS walkie-talkies, and NOAA weather radio receivers.	Provides various communication options for different scenarios and weather updates.
Integrate a shortwave receiver.	Install a shortwave receiver in your vehicle to monitor international broadcasts.	Access to international news and emergency information, broadening your communication scope.

Chapter 7
Mobility And Evacuation Plans

| Establish protocols for checking in and sharing information | Develop protocols within your network for checking in and sharing critical information. | Ensures effective communication and coordination within your network during emergencies. |

To allow for more HAM radios, improved energy lines and emergency inverters are necessary. By making some advance plans or arrangements, your civilian automobile will be at the same level for speed in its maximum operation condition, alone or with other vehicles. It will be very dependable and have good communication too.

Shall we converse on a hypothetical scenario about the emergency of your motorcar? You are driving out to escape an approaching calamity. Still, unfortunately, as fate would have it, your well-serviced petrol guzzler's battery goes off for no apparent reason, and now you're stuck in the middle of nowhere alone. What measures will you employ to ensure that your lorry's engine functions again?

Step-by-Step Guide:

Step 1: Assess the Situation

Remain calm and move your truck off the road to a safe shoulder area if possible.

Step 2: Ensure Safety

Ensure proper safety precautions by setting up road flares, triangles, or warning lights to alert other drivers.

Step 3: Access Emergency Kit

Access your truck's emergency kit and any specialty automotive tools you've prepared for this situation.

Step 4: Inspect Battery Connections

Visually inspect the battery connections, ensuring they are clean and securely tightened.

Step 5: Diagnose Battery Issue

By checking other electrical components, determine if the battery is truly dead or if another electrical failure is causing the issue.

Step 6: Remove Old Battery

If the battery fails, use your jack and wrenches to remove it from the engine bay.

Vehicle Preparedness And Maintenance
The Ultimate Prepper's Survival Bible

Step 7: Install Replacement Battery

Properly install your backup replacement battery and securely connect all terminals.

Step 8: Utilize Backup Electrical System

If your truck has a backup electrical reserve, switch to that system to start it up.

Step 9: Connect the Backup Power Source

If no backup systems are available, locate and safely connect your backup portable power source to jump-start the truck.

Step 10: Monitor and Proceed

Once the truck runs, closely monitor instrumentation for any irregularities and proceed to the nearest service center for a thorough inspection and potential replacement of the main battery.

Vehicle Emergency Checklist

Item	Quantity	Purpose	Notes
Backup Battery	1	Replacement	Proper group size
Jumper Cables	1 set	Engine start	Four gauges, 20 ft length
Jack & Lug Wrench	1 each	Tire/battery changes	Match your vehicle
Jump Starter	1	Portable power	Lithium battery preferred
Multimeter	1	Diagnose electrical	DVOM for voltage testing
Fuse Assortment	1 kit	Replacement fuses	Include fuse pullers
Code Reader	1	Check engine codes	OBD2 Bluetooth enabled
Battery Terminal Kit	1	Clean connections	Wire brushes, protector spray
Mechanics Gloves	Two pairs	Safety/grip	Chemical resistant
Emergency Markers	Variety	Visibility/warning	Flares, triangles, LED beacons

Chapter 7
Mobility And Evacuation Plans

Basic Tool Kit	1	Field repairs	Wrenches, sockets, pliers, hammer
Fix-A-Flat	Two cans	Temporary inflation	Coats and seals tires
Portable Air Compressor	1	Inflate tires	12V, high volume output
Tire Plug Kit	1	Long term repairs	Plugs and reaming tools

Keeping your vehicle in good working order is extremely important for emergencies. Regular maintenance helps ensure reliable transportation when you need it most. There are some additional preparations you can make to your vehicle as well.

Strategies for Surviving on the Move

In major crises, you may need to leave your home for extended periods. Being forced to relocate or constantly move to find safety temporarily requires special strategies and preparation.

Conserve fuel as much as possible by combining trips and avoiding excessive engine idling. Keep vehicles well-tuned and tires properly inflated for efficiency. Siphon gas from other vehicles if necessary.

Monitor news and official communication channels for safe travel routes and location updates. Unexpected detours may become required if certain areas become too hazardous.

Pack only the essential supplies needed to sustain you and your group while actively traveling:

- Water and high-calorie, non-perishable food
- Warm, multi-layer clothing for all weather
- Hygiene and sanitation items
- Basic tools, utensils, cookware
- Self-powered communication/navigation devices

Condense and lighten your load as much as possible for mobile efficiency. You may need to temporarily cache or bury heavier supply caches in secure locations for later retrieval.

Always prioritize your security and avoid drawing attention. Use tactics like:

Strategies for Surviving on the Move
The Ultimate Prepper's Survival Bible

- Traveling only during daylight if possible
- Concealing or camouflaging your vehicles
- Varying routes and avoiding patterns
- Circumventing any populated areas
- Properly fortifying any campsites

Foraging and Hunting Food

It is important to safely acquire food from the wild when one has to stay alive. Therefore, it would be intelligent to learn and hone such ancestral capabilities in advance:

Skill	Description	Importance
Wild Edible Plants	Study guidebooks to identify plants, roots, nuts, and berries that are safe to consume in your region. Know their seasonality.	Vital for sustenance
Trapping Small Game	Construct basic snares using rope, wire, or natural materials to catch rabbits, squirrels, and other small prey.	Important for protein sources
Primitive Hunting	Practice remote hunting techniques like making spears, bows/arrows, or slingshots from materials in your environment.	Provides alternative food
Water Sources	Seek out and properly treat any found water sources when traveling, as potable drinking water is more critical than survival food.	Essential for hydration

Water Procurement	Description	Importance

Chapter 7
Mobility And Evacuation Plans

Strategy		
Travel Near Water Sources	Use maps and geography knowledge to plan travel routes near potential water sources like rivers, lakes, and streams whenever possible.	Essential for water availability
Carry Water Purification Methods	Carry portable water filters, purification tablets, or a way to boil/disinfect any collected water before consuming it to ensure it's safe to drink.	Vital for preventing waterborne diseases
Identify Natural Springs	Know markers for identifying different types of natural springs, as they can be a reliable water source if properly treated.	Valuable for accessing clean water
Craft Solar Still in Coastal Areas	Develop skills to make a simple solar still that can collect drinking water from the sea and other salty waters. This is important in areas along the coast as there may be few alternatives for obtaining fresh drinking water.	Useful for obtaining drinkable water from saltwater sources

Concealment and Camouflage

To lower the probability of being seen by any dangerous people while walking, blending well with the environment is advisable. Become an expert in techniques such as:

Stealth Tactics	Description	Importance
Utilize Natural Cover	Using natural vegetation, debris, and terrain features to obscure positions and travel paths reduces visibility to potential threats.	Essential for minimizing detection
Wear Camouflage	Disrupt recognizable human form outlines by wearing camouflage patterns and ghillie suit pieces, blending in with the surrounding environment.	Crucial for avoiding visual detection
Control Light, Noise, and	Carefully control light, noise, and any other signatures that could expose your group's	Vital for maintaining operational security

Signatures	location, maintaining stealth and minimizing the risk of detection.	
Vary Travel Patterns	Vary travel schedules, routes, and campsites to avoid establishing detectable patterns, making it harder for adversaries to predict your movements.	It is important for preventing tracking and ambush

Cryptic Communication

In case of separation during movement, develop secret codes, words, and signals for clandestine communication between yourselves. Examples:

- There will be symbolic graffiti made using dirt and organic paints on the paths, showing which way should be followed.
- The planned-out secretive signs include information on where to go, what is available there, and what should be avoided but look casual. They are left in the form of chalk lines or slight traces that can only be seen by attentive eyes but not noticed by most people.

Environmental Survival

It is important to acquire certain skills on how to stay safe, find your way, communicate, and identify danger while changing position in different regions due to the climatic situations:

- Desert - Seeking protection from the sun, keeping hydrated, defensive postures
- Extreme Cold - Keeping warm, preventing frostbite and hypothermia injuries.
- Tropical Rainforest - Cleanliness, harmless flora/fauna species, sleeping on hammocks.

We can consider an EMP incident that has paralyzed the electricity grids and other related amenities in many states within the US. There will be no time for relaxation since even the backup plans will fail to operate when the few fuels available are finished, and people are left with nothing to rely on.

In this case, your extended family opts to move out of the area for good; they plan on going to a safe place that can provide for itself about some hundreds of miles from there. If you were going to make it through this adventure, what tactics are we using?

Chapter 7
Mobility And Evacuation Plans

Step-by-Step Guide:

<u>Step 1: Prepare the Team</u>

Equip every member with high-standard backpacks, tough bivouac equipment, water filters/purifiers, and simple weapons for self-defense.

<u>Step 2: Get Complex Charts</u>

Acquire accurate maps that indicate possible water sources, such as rivers and lakes, during your passage to guarantee a way of getting important drinks.

<u>Step 3: Store Supplies Safely</u>

At predetermined points on the route, keep sealed supply buckets containing non-perishable food and supplies intended for emergencies.

<u>Step 4: Study How to Stay Alive</u>

Study the edible plants found in the region, as well as trapping techniques and primitive hunting methods that could be used in addition to the foodstuffs obtained to ensure the continued existence of the food.

<u>Step 5: Remember Signs and Signals</u>

Memorize discreet trail signs, including simple coded messages or symbols that would show how you are traveling but not attract attention.

<u>Step 6: Move Stealthily</u>

Move under cover of darkness wearing ghillie suits or other camouflage clothing and paint for detection-beating purposes when traveling across open country undetected.

<u>Step 7: Change Camping Locations</u>

Change camp locations daily far from main travel paths to avoid being trailed by other people. Ensure proper covering of all fires and luminous points so operational safety is not compromised.

<u>Step 8: Assign Lookouts</u>

Assign armed sentry who should be changing after some time to monitor whether there are any enemies nearby, especially when they are taking some rest; this will help them ensure that their security is enhanced during such resting periods throughout their journey.

<u>Step 9: Reconvene Within Safe Zones</u>

Strategies for Surviving on the Move
The Ultimate Prepper's Survival Bible

If they lose touch, they should come together again at agreed-upon rallying places using secret communication codes to organize reunion attempts.

Long-Term Survival Mobility Checklist

Item	Quantity	Purpose	Notes
Backpacks	1 per person	Carry all gear	Rugged, framed
Bivouac Sacks	1 per person	Sleeping insulation	Breathable, weather-resistant
Water Filters	2-3	Potable water	Portable, high-capacity
Water Purification	200+ tablets	Disinfect water	Chlorine dioxide or iodine
Map Case	1	Secure map storage	Waterproof, tear-resistant
Signaling Mirror	1 per group	Emergency comms	Unbreakable, high-visibility
Camouflage	1 outfit per person	Concealment	Breathable ghillie suits, face paint
Multipurpose Tool	1 per person	Field tools	Fixed/folding blade, pliers, saw
Trekking Poles	1 pair per person	Rugged terrain	Adjustable anti-shock
Solar Charger	2	Recharge devices	Guided for positioning
Loud Whistle	1 per person	Signaling	Pea-less for reliability
Lightweight Trowel	1 per person	Slit trenches	Collapsible, compact
Personal Light	1 per person	Navigation	Headlamp or chemlight
Cash Currency	$100 per person	Temporary resupply	Mixed larger/smaller bills

During a crisis, the knowledge of leaving places and their appropriate destinations can save lives.

Chapter 7
Mobility And Evacuation Plans

When evacuation routes are made known while rally points are determined, one can evacuate everyone quickly when trouble arises but in an orderly fashion.

Don't forget to gather important materials, know what's happening around you, and keep safe first. By thinking ahead and getting ready for the worst, you'll face any difficult situation head-on and bounce back.

What if you need to leave in a hurry? Financial preparedness is a key element that provides you with more options and a sense of security. In the next chapter, I'll share insider tips on resource stockpiling, trading skills, and even creative financial management, ensuring you have a financial safety net. With these strategies, you can take the necessary steps to ensure your safety and your family's.

CHAPTER 8
FINANCIAL PREPAREDNESS

Having a solid financial plan can make a difference in times of crisis. Preparing financially for a natural disaster, economic downturn, or global pandemic can help you and your family weather the storm.

This chapter will explore the economic impact of crises, strategies for managing your finances during uncertain times, and the importance of bartering and trading in a post-disaster economy.

Economic Impact of a Crisis

In times of crisis, the economic consequences of unfortunate events cannot be undermined. Such occurrences may lead to unemployment, inflation, and difficulty accessing commodities.

At such moments, one should particularly appreciate why this affects the financial position. It's crucial to learn from any economic disaster to prepare yourself.

Knowing the risks and challenges, what can you do to ensure your money is safe and properly prepared for such a difficult period?

Suppose there is an economic crisis across the nation with very negative effects. Many people are out of employment, and consumer spending is down.

Lots of companies went out of business, and the stock exchange index fell significantly in many cases. How could one plan for this?

Step-by-Step Guide

Preparing yourself becomes crucial whenever the economy is going through a bad phase. Take note of these straightforward measures that you follow:

Step 1: Save up an emergency fund.

Try saving some cash, which should be around six months of living expenses, i.e., rent, electricity bills, groceries, etc., in a safe place that is easily accessible, probably a savings account.

Step 2: Cut back on spending on things you don't need.

See where to spend less, such as restaurant outings, entertainment, and low subscribed services.

Step 3: Find ways to make some extra money on the side.

Chapter 8
Financial Preparedness

Maybe you can secure employment for a few hours or kick-start a small business based on your skills, such as gardening, making cards, typing online, etc.

Step 4: Be smart about investing.

In times like these, the stock market may experience high volatility. Research about commodities and non-depreciating assets, e.g., gold and land, with a slower devaluation rate than currency.

Step 5: Stock up on essentials you'll need.

Ensure the availability of non-perishable foods, cans of bottled water, and other vital commodities even when it is difficult to buy them because supply is disrupted.

Step 6: Learn useful skills

It would be great if you could learn some educational lessons that can help you earn extra cash or help you handle emergency issues by yourself. For instance, gardening knowledge, simple house fixing ability, or carpentry education is very important.

Step 7: Stay up-to-date on economic news

Keep yourself informed about economic matters and also listen to professionals' opinions. Such information will assist you in making sane decisions regarding your monetary circumstances.

Step 8: Talk to a financial advisor

Consider seeking a financial expert who can analyze your unique position and offer advice on surviving during this difficult time with your family.

Taking steps in advance, lowering expenses, finding ways for self-employment, and assisting others may be crucial keys when there is a threat to your economy.

Checklist

Item	Quantity	Notes
Emergency Fund	Six months' worth of expenses	Keep a secure, easily accessible account
Stockpiled Food	3-6 months' supply	Non-perishable, nutritious items
Stockpiled Water	1 gallon per person per day	For drinking, cooking, and hygiene

Economic Impact of a Crisis
The Ultimate Prepper's Survival Bible

| Alternative Income Sources | As needed | Side gigs, small businesses, or freelance work |

Supply Chain Disruptions

Let's say a big natural disaster damages factories and roads, making it hard to get things we use every day. How would you get ready for and deal with being unable to get those things?

Step-by-Step Guide

Here are some simple steps to get ready for shortages:

1. Stock up on essentials like non-perishable foods, water, and medicine, so you have enough for a while.
2. Find local and nearby places to get important supplies, not just big chains.
3. Look into carpooling, biking, or community groups to help move things around if roads are blocked.
4. Grow your food, collect rainwater, or make your energy.
5. Support local businesses and farmers to strengthen your community's ability to provide for itself.
6. Learn to fix and maintain things yourself so they last longer.
7. Share, trade, or rent items with others instead of buying new ones.

Stay up-to-date on supply issues and be ready to change your plans as needed. Being flexible and resourceful is key when shortages happen.

Checklist

Item	Description	Purpose	Notes
Emergency Stockpile	Non-perishable food, water, medical supplies	Ensure immediate needs are met	Rotate and replenish regularly
Local Sourcing Options	Regional suppliers, farmers' markets	Diversify supply sources	Build relationships and networks
Alternative	Carpooling, bicycle	Reduce reliance on	Explore

Chapter 8
Financial Preparedness

Transportation	delivery	traditional logistics	community-based solutions
Self-Sufficiency Practices	Growing food, harvesting rainwater, renewable energy	Increase self-reliance	Research and implement gradually
Repair and Maintenance Skills	Basic repairs, equipment maintenance	Extend the life of goods	Attend workshops or online tutorials
Sharing Economy	Barter, trade, rental systems	Access resources without ownership	Participate in community initiatives

Manage Finances in Uncertain Times

If you don't have much money, there are some ways through which you can take care of your financial situation. Planning for your money; keep track of what you owe and pay towards it. Watch out for opportunities for profitable investment or additional earnings. With these in mind, one will be at ease and adaptable.

One should ensure that one employs appropriate monetary policies even when things are tough financially. Doing this can assist one to remain steady now, worry little about tomorrow, and recover with pace later on.

Imagine a scenario whereby commodities are depleted due to a worldwide disease pandemic, hence pushing up prices. Several firms underwent mass retrenchment procedures. If you were in such a situation, how could you cope?

Follow the given procedure:

This is what you should do step by step to take care of your money when the going gets rough:

Step 1: Update Your Budget

Revise your budget so that it reflects your fresh earnings and outgoings. Start with priority spending on things such as accommodation, food, etc.

Step 2: Cut Unnecessary Spending

Cease spending on irrelevant goods like subscriptions, take-outs, and fun, among others, so that you can save some money.

Manage Finances in Uncertain Times
The Ultimate Prepper's Survival Bible

Step 3: Communicate with Creditors

Contact lenders, including those associated with credit cards and electricity/water/gas bills. Most creditors have special payment relief programs available during emergencies.

Step 4: Find Extra Income

Explore other income opportunities such as getting temporary employment, doing freelance work, or beginning an online business.

Step 5: Apply for Government Assistance

Confirm whether you meet the eligibility criteria stipulated in public aid initiatives similar to social insurance packages or economic stimulus funds that can help you foot the bills.

Step 6: Prioritize Debt Repayment

Repay high-rate loans first while maintaining minimum installments on cheap ones to reduce total loan volume.

Step 7: Maintain Emergency Savings

If possible, continue adding to your emergency savings fund for a financial back-up.

Step 8: Seek Professional Advice

Consider meeting with a financial advisor who can provide personalized advice tailored to your situation. The key is adjusting your spending, finding new income, and using helpful programs. Having a plan makes getting through money troubles easier. Don't be afraid to ask for help too.

Checklist

Item	Quantity/Timeframe	Purpose
Emergency Fund	3-6 months' worth of expenses	Financial safety net
Debt Repayment Plan	Monthly payments	Prioritize high-interest debt
Budget Review	Monthly or as needed	Adjust for changes in income/expenses
Alternative Income Sources	As needed	Supplement primary income

Chapter 8
Financial Preparedness

Create Multiple Income Streams

It's really smart to have money coming from different places. If you lose one job or income source, you still have other ways to make money. Having multiple income streams makes you prepared for hard times.

Multiple income streams are important because they protect you if you suddenly can't work your main job or your business struggles. If you have other money, you can still pay for housing, food, and other needs.

Let's say there is a bad recession, and many people lose jobs or businesses close down. Your main income is impacted, and it's hard to pay bills. What could you do to create extra sources of income to get through the tough times?

Step-by-Step Guide

Step 1: Assess Your Skills and Resources

Analyze your abilities, hobbies, and propertyton see any potential money-making chance that matches what you are good at.

Step 2: Start a Side Business or Freelance

Think about beginning a part-time job or freelancing in sectors that require knowledge in them, e. g., counseling or academics.

Step 3: Explore Passive Income Sources

Investigate how to earn money without being actively involved, e.g., through rental business, affiliate marketing, and creating digital commodities such as e-books.

Step 4: Look for Part-Time or Gig Work

Search for extra jobs or gigs to boost your monthly earnings, like driving for ride-hailing apps, doing deliveries, or engaging in online freelance work.

Step 5: Monetize Hobbies or Talents

You can make money from your talents or hobbies by using platforms like Etsy and Fiverr and participating in local trade events.

Step 6: Invest in Income-Producing Assets

Put your funds into assets that bring money, such as stocks that pay dividends, corporate bonds, p2p lending, etc., creating more income sources.

Step 7: Continuously Seek New Opportunities

Always look for new chances, be ready to change, and acquire more skills because the environment is changing and evolving daily; thus, one must remain competitive.

Step 8: Prioritize and Allocate Time and Resources

Arrange your priorities well and apportion your time plus other resources appropriately among the different businesses so you can get high output and income from all of them.

Checklist

Item	Description	Purpose	Notes
Skills Inventory	List of your skills and expertise	Identify income opportunities	Update regularly
Side Business Plan	Business model, target market, pricing	Generate additional income	Scalable and sustainable
Passive Income Sources	Rental properties, digital products, etc.	Recurring income streams	Requires upfront investment
Gig Work Platforms	Rideshare, delivery, online tasks	Flexible income sources	Requires reliable transportation or technology
Creative Outlets	Etsy, Fiverr, local craft fairs	Monetize hobbies and talents	Leverage existing skills and interests

Negotiate Debt and Payment Plans

Discussing with lenders and utility companies may give you some respite and enhance control of loans and expenses when going through a financial crisis.

Re-arranging debt and payment plans will keep one away from additional charges, penalties, or lawsuits while allowing them to keep their focus on important bills and stay financially afloat.

Suppose there was a tragedy at your residence, leading to massive destruction and loss of business. Right now, you cannot even manage because there is too much mortgage to pay, yet you don't know where to get money for food and other necessities because you have been fired. In such a difficult period, how could you approach your creditors and service providers to handle

Chapter 8
Financial Preparedness

the issue of debts and expenses?

Step-by-Step Guide

Step 1: Prioritize Your Debts and Expenses

Begin by giving priority to what you owe as well as what you spend.

Step 2: Contact Creditors and Service Providers

Communicate with your creditors and service providers promptly regarding your current predicament and ask for an emergency relief package or a payment plan to help you meet your obligations now.

Step 3: Gather Documentation

Ensure you gather documentation showing why it has been difficult financially for you, such as unemployment records, hospital bills, or anything else that can prove valid reasons for claiming that.

Checklist

Item	Description	Purpose	Notes
Debt Prioritization	Essential vs. non-essential debts	Focus on critical expenses	Avoid defaults and late fees
Hardship Documentation	Proof of financial hardship	Support negotiations	Job loss, medical bills, disaster expenses
Negotiation Strategies	Lower interest rates, deferred payments, etc.	Ease financial burden	Be prepared to compromise.
Debt Consolidation Options	Combine multiple debts into one payment	Simplify debt management	Evaluate terms and fees
Written Agreements	Documented payment plans and arrangements	Ensure clarity and accountability	Avoid misunderstandings

Manage Finances in Uncertain Times
The Ultimate Prepper's Survival Bible

Build an Emergency Fund

If you set some money aside for emergencies, you will be financially safe even if anything tragic happens. This money is meant to help care for your basic needs in case anything goes wrong. It may save you from getting into loans and consuming all of your savings.

It does not make sense to assume that a person who has set an emergency fund can fail to survive through periods such as economic depression, where people lose jobs. We experience situations when there are no goods in shops due to COVID-19, and it leads to crises all over the world. The fact is, many companies have experienced downsizing or laying off employees due to this reason. So, if you ever face difficulties like losing your job and being unable to meet various financial obligations, ask yourself one question: Can an emergency fund provide any assistance during this economic meltdown?

Step-by-Step Guide

Step 1: Determine Essential Monthly Expenses

To know the basic money you need monthly, first find out some of your necessary monthly expenses, such as housing, food, utilities, and transportation.

Step 2: Establish a Savings Goal

Ensure you set aside some money for a difficult period, equal to savings for at least three to six months. Doing this every month will give you enough money even in financial trouble.

Step 3: Set Up a Dedicated Savings Account

Establish a distinct bank account or money market fund for your emergency cash reserve.

Step 4: Automate Regular Transfers

To ensure your savings keep growing steadily, you should automate transferring certain sums or making contributions to your emergency fund every month, even if they are very small.

Step 5: Boost Your Savings

Seek ways of increasing your savings for emergencies, which could be advancing your goal using tax refunds, bonuses, or money earned from extra jobs.

Step 6: Resist Non-Essential Withdrawals

Don't be tempted to use your emergency money for things you don't need or are luxurious. Keep it for when you'll need it.

Step 7: Review and Adjust Periodically

Chapter 8
Financial Preparedness

To ensure that your savings goal for emergency funds is enough, you should review and modify it from time to time regarding changes in expenses or situations.

Checklist

Item	Description	Purpose	Notes
Essential Expenses Calculation	Monthly costs for housing, food, utilities, etc.	Determine emergency fund goal.	Update regularly
Dedicated Savings Account	A separate account for an emergency fund	Avoid dipping into other savings	High-yield account preferred
Automated Contributions	Recurring transfers or payroll deductions	Consistent savings habit	Adjust as needed
Side Income Sources	Freelancing, gig work, selling items	Boost emergency fund savings	Temporary or occasional
Investment Options	Low-risk, liquid investments	Grow emergency fund over time	Avoid high-risk or illiquid investments

Barter and Trade in a Post-Disaster Economy

Knowledge of how trade and swap work will enable one to get important commodities and services even during malfunctioning economic exchange. This way, one can use what he has, like talents, skills, or properties, among others.

Suppose there was a massive blackout that lasted for days in your town. Conventional monetary units have very low demand, while most commodities and services cannot be found easily. In such a case, can a bazaar help you go through safely, and if so, what should you do?

Step-By-Step Guide:

First Step: Determine Your Skills And What You Have

Write down the abilities, talents, and property you think would matter when exchanging goods or services in a barter trade.

Second Step – Create Links

Barter and Trade in a Post-Disaster Economy
The Ultimate Prepper's Survival Bible

Establish communication channels with other community members who may want to engage in barter or trade.

Third Step – Set Up A Barter System

Agree upon a just and uniform method of appraising commodities and services exchanged through barters like measurement units taken across the board or point system.

Fourth Step – Engage In Exchange Of Merchandise

Involve yourself in non-complex exchanges where you gain experience and create confidence among network members.

Fifth Step: Keep Records

Ensure that you have written everything about any exchange or pact made so that justice can prevail without favoritism on anyone's side.

Sixth step: Adapt easily and broadminded

Be ready to change positions and discuss matters as the situation demands.

Seventh Step: Ensure Safekeeping Of All Involved Parties

Take utmost care, including necessary measures, while involved in trade by the batter, especially with strangers or in unknown conditions.

Checklist

Item	Description	Purpose	Notes
Barter Goods	Non-perishable food, tools, hygiene products, etc.	For trading	Stockpile valuable items
Skills and Resources	Carpentry, gardening, medical knowledge, etc.	For trading services	Identify your strengths
Barter Network	Local community members interested in bartering	For establishing trust and connections	Build relationships
Standardized System	Unit of measurement, points system, etc.	For fair valuation of goods/services	Agree on a system

Chapter 8
Financial Preparedness

Identifying High-Value Barter Items

Your ability to trade for what you want can be enhanced by possessing many valuable goods for exchange that other people may wish to have.

Consider an extreme lack of rain in the area; hence, many crops have failed, and there is insufficient water. People no longer value normal money because they use every means possible to get food and clean drinking water. What ways could you use to accumulate enough commodities to be easily traded in a time of need so that your family lives without problems?

Step-by-Step Guide

1. Conduct a study and determine what people need most when there is insufficient water, e.g., canned foods, tablets for purifying drinking water, seeds or gardening equipment, and equipment to collect or distribute water.
2. Accumulate these commodities by buying them at discounted prices or cheaply whenever possible.
3. Ensure you keep your trade items safe from moisture in a suitable place, taking all necessary measures to increase their durability.
4. Have a record of the number and state of commodities in your trade storage.
5. Expect to exchange extra goods for ones you lack during the dry period; therefore, be prepared.

Checklist

Item	Quantity	Purpose	Notes
Non-perishable Food	6-12 months' supply	Food source	Canned goods, grains, etc.
Water Purification Tablets	1,000+ tablets	Clean drinking water	Chlorine dioxide or iodine
Seeds	Assorted varieties	Growing food	Heirloom, non-hybrid
Gardening Tools	Shovels, hoes, etc.	Cultivation	Durable, long-lasting
Water Collection	5-10 gallon	Storing water	Clean, food-grade

Containers	capacity		

Establishing a Barter Network

Suppose the biggest earthquake ever experienced hits your town, resulting in massive destruction and the breakdown of basic facilities. After the event, there will be many goods, but little will be left for trade as very little shall follow the usual channel. How, then, can you plan on having a barter system so that when it comes back, your community can get on its feet again and take care of itself?

Step-By-Step Plan

<u>Stage 1: Determine Prospective Participants</u>

Point out some persons or organizations within the locality that may create a basis for exchange through their activities.

<u>Stage 2: Arrange Meeting</u>

Plan for a meeting whereby people can discuss how beneficial trading systems could be and then set some fair-trade rules within which barter network should operate.

<u>Stage 3: Make a List of Exchange Media</u>

Compile an electronic or paper-based record containing details about group members, such as their competencies, wealth, and requirements, making pairing easier.

<u>Stage 4: Develop Ways of Assigning Value</u>

Create an appraisal mechanism for commodities and services, e.g., using points or standardized units, promoting equal transactions.

<u>Stage 5: Circulate Data</u>

Tell those in the network to tell other members what they have too much of now, what is needed most, and where it could be traded quickly.

<u>Stage 6: Assist With Trade</u>

Ensure just and open exchange of swaps and other trades between network members while monitoring involvement through honest means to maintain trust.

<u>Stage 7: Choose Intermediaries</u>

Think about selecting someone trusted or even forming a committee tasked with handling disagreements among yourselves so they are resolved amicably.

Chapter 8
Financial Preparedness

<u>Step 8: Encourage Togetherness</u>

Promote society and cooperation by arranging communal events like collective farming or teaching various skills; this will tighten relationships among people.

<u>Step 9: Create Links With Others</u>

Consider accepting new members into the network and relating with neighboring societies or organizations so that a wider range of commodities and opportunities can be available for trade.

Checklist

Item	Description	Purpose	Notes
Network Members	Local individuals/groups	Participate in bartering	Maintain a database
Barter Guidelines	Rules and regulations	Ensure fair trade	Establish collectively
Valuation System	Point-based, standardized unit	Assign values to goods/services	Agree on a system
Communication Channels	Meetings, forums, etc.	Share information and needs	Foster transparency
Dispute Resolution	Mediation process	Address conflicts	Appoint trusted individuals

To sum up, getting ready for any emergency requires that individuals are well prepared financially. This can be achieved through comprehending the financial implications of emergencies, creating financial plans, and being open to trade and exchange as an alternative transaction means. It is important to remember that to stay safe during times of doubt, you must take initiative and be willing to change and adjust when necessary.

Money's important, no doubt, but what's even more vital? A strong mindset. Having all the supplies and plans in the world will mean something other than squatting if you mentally crack under pressure. That's why the next chapter focuses on psychological preparedness - fortifying your mind just as much as your bunker. With my field-tested techniques, you'll build the unshakable resolve to survive and overcome any traumatic situation.

CHAPTER 9
PSYCHOLOGICAL PREPAREDNESS

It is important to have more than just the appropriate supplies and equipment to be prepared for unforeseen circumstances. One should also prepare himself psychologically and emotionally for tough conditions.

In this chapter, we will cover some methods that can help one deal with stress and panic while trying to become tougher to think positively and increase the chances of staying alive.

Coping Strategies for Stress and Anxiety

It is natural for you to get anxious or develop stress when an emergency strikes. Feeling uneasy and frightened is typical; however, there are ways of dealing with these emotions to prevent them from taking over you completely. Consider these hints on how to handle pressure and fear:

- Deep breathing exercises can help you relax. Breathe slowly and deeply through your nose and out through your mouth.
- Remember, you're not alone. Many people experience stress in difficult situations.

Checklist: Coping With Stress

Breathing Exercises	Meditation/Mindfulness	Exercise
Deep breaths	Find a quiet space	Walk or stretch
Inhale through nose	Clear your mind	Do yoga
Exhale through mouth	Focus on the present	Lift light weights
Repeat slowly	Let thoughts pass	Get your heart pumping

Crisis Scenario: At the park, Sam played happily until he heard a loud sound. Strong winds blew; trees fell. People began running away to safety. In all this confusion, Sam lost sight of his parents. He felt very scared and alone.

This is how Sam should act:

Step 1: Stay calm

Chapter 9
Psychological Preparedness

Getting hysterical won't do any good. Inhale deeply so that you can maintain yourself together.

<u>Step 2: Find a Safe Place</u>

Identify somewhere secure where he can stay, such as inside any building or nearby car.

<u>Step 3: Seek Help from a Trusted Adult</u>

Tell them to call for help from an officer or guard in case they get separated from them at the park.

<u>Step 4: Provide Important Details</u>

Tell them some important facts about the child, e. g., name(s), parents, name, and phone number(s).

<u>Step 5: Wait Patiently</u>

Stay cool and collected; bide your time. His parents would go all out searching for their child, and they would spot him with the support offered.

<u>Step 6: Reunite and Communicate</u>

After the reunion, recount the event truthfully, but do not dwell upon bad emotions.

Mental Health Strategies for Surviving Crisis Situations

Feeling scared, worried, or sad is common if the worst happens and should be expected; however, such emotions are alright. One's psychological welfare should also be attended to.

Below are a few suggestions that can assist you in improving your mood:

- Spend time talking to family and friends. Let them know how you feel. Hugs can make you feel better, too!
- Do things that make you happy and relaxed. Read your favorite book. Listen to calm music. Color or draw pictures. These fun activities get your mind off worries.
- Move your body! Go for a walk outside. Run and play active games if it's safe. Getting exercise helps let out energy and worries.
- Keep living spaces clean and comfortable. Make your home pretty with things that make you smile—Cuddle with a stuffed animal or pet.
- When you feel worried, try taking deep, slow breaths. Breathe in through your nose, out through your mouth. Feeling your belly go in and out can help calm your mind.
- Don't forget to eat, drink water, and get plenty of sleep. Our minds and bodies need food and rest to stay healthy, especially in hard times.

Coping Strategies for Stress and Anxiety
The Ultimate Prepper's Survival Bible

- Be kind and patient with yourself and others. Hard days will eventually end. Focus on doing small, good things for as long as you need to get through it.
- Staying strong in your mind will help you be ready for anything that comes your way. Remember, you've got this!

Crisis Scenario: A devastating tornado has destroyed many homes in your town, including yours. While you and your family are physically unharmed, the loss is overwhelming. How can you take care of your mental health during this traumatic time?

Step-by-Step Guide

1. Find a safe place to temporarily relocate your family - with relatives, at a shelter, etc.
2. Once settled, allow yourselves to talk openly about the tornado and how you feel. Let emotions out.
3. Re-establish routines around meals, bedtimes, and other daily activities to provide comfort.
4. Spend quality time together doing simple activities you enjoy - games, reading, crafting.
5. If you have kids, encourage them to express feelings through drawing, writing stories, or playing.
6. Build in regular physical activity like walking around the neighborhood to reduce stress.
7. Limit excess news/media that triggers trauma and anxiety. Take breaks from the difficult realities.
8. Help out other community members when you can - giving support allows healing.
9. Seek professional counseling if overwhelming sadness, anxiety, or other struggles persist.
10. Be patient and kind with yourselves and each other throughout the challenging recovery process.

Chapter 9
Psychological Preparedness

Checklist: Mental Health

Item	Purpose	Notes
Journal/Notebook	Expressing feelings	Bring pens/pencils
Portable Game/Toys	Enjoyable distractions	Travel games, cards, etc.
Inspiring Reading	Uplift mood	Motivational or spiritual texts
Stuffed Animal	Comfort item	Especially for children
Portable Music Player	Calming influences	Preload soothing playlists
Mindfulness App	Relaxation exercises	For meditation, deep breathing
Family Photos	Cherished memories	Put in a waterproof sleeve

If you have faith, read uplifting religious or spiritual texts. Pray or study writings that remind you of hope, inner strength, and higher purposes during hardship. Staying spiritually grounded brings comfort.

Spending time outdoors can boost your mental well-being, even briefly. Take a short walk, do gentle stretches, or sit outside.

Your family cannot leave the house because of a very strong winter and no heat or electricity. The forecast predicts that it will be below zero for many weeks, and this makes you think about how people in the house will feel, and maybe they will even go crazy from this increased stress and anxiety. What can you do to keep their sanity intact?

Step-by-Step Guide

Step 1: Gather Supplies

Collect journals, art supplies, spiritual readings, and battery-operated stereo/radios.

Step 2: Create a Family "Quiet Space"

Make special areas where everyone can easily have privacy using comforters or screens.

Step 3: Read Aloud

Alternatively, read passages derived from motivational literature or recount hilarious and inspiring anecdotes.

Coping Strategies for Stress and Anxiety
The Ultimate Prepper's Survival Bible

Step 4: Allocate Alone Time for Each Individual.

Assign particular moments daily for separate personal space or silent contemplation.

Step 5: Engage in Calm Music Orchestration and Physical Education

Employ low-intensity soothing music and involve yourselves in group mild stretches or breath control exercises.

Step 6: Take Breaks Outside

Take short breaks outside to breathe fresh air and enjoy the environment if possible and safe.

Step 7: Keep in Touch with Others

Whenever feasible, utilize video calls to maintain contact with extended family members.

Step 8: Encourage and Remind

Tell them they are not alone in facing these challenges and remind them they are only temporary; also, plan some fun games!

Step 9: Dealing With Pressure

In case of heightened tensions, remain calm and take a brief timeout away from the scene.

Step 10: Stick To Routine

Maintain regular day-to-day routine, including mealtimes, chores, and sleep, to ensure a sense of normalcy/stability.

Checklist: Mental Health

Item	Quantity	Purpose	Notes
Journal/Notebook	1 per person	Writing out emotions	Get fun designs
Coloring Books	4-5	Relaxing creative outlet	For kids and adults
Craft Supplies	Assortment	DIY projects	Yarn, wood, paints, etc.
Portable Music Player	1-2	Calming music therapy	Preloaded playlists
Deck of Cards	2	Play games together	For mental breaks
Spiritual Readings	2-3 books	Inspiration/Perspective	Religious or

Chapter 9
Psychological Preparedness

			philosophical
Candles/Lamp Oil	1 month supply	Peaceful lighting	Avoid open flames
Blankets/Pillows	2-3 per person	Cozy, quiet space	Add sheets for partitions
Puzzles/Board Games	3-4	Engaging distractions	Mix of types
Warm Beverages	Ample supplies	Comfort and routine	Teas, hot chocolate
Notebook/Pen	1 per person	Goal setting	Allow hope and planning

Develop Resilience in Crisis Situations

Surviving tough situations requires one to possess the capability of recovering quickly from them. This is a necessary trait for emergency survival. The following are some methods of increasing resilience:

One should accept the fact that, at times, life is never certain or smooth. With such an attitude, you will be able to adapt to any situation without much stress or frustration.

Checklist: Building Resilience

Support Network	Self-Care	Problem-Solving
Family members	Nutritious diet	Break issues into steps
Close friends	Adequate sleep	Consider all options
Community groups	Relaxation time	Ask for help when needed
Co-workers	Exercise routine	Learn from setbacks

After a fierce ice storm, the Johnson family's neighborhood lost electricity for many days. They couldn't warm their house, cook, or charge anything due to lack of electricity. Despite being

Develop Resilience in Crisis Situations
The Ultimate Prepper's Survival Bible

under pressure, the Johnsons remained strong.

Here's what they did:

1. Used emergency supplies like blankets, warm clothes, non-perishable foods, and battery-powered lights.
2. Checked on elderly neighbors, sharing supplies and offering company.
3. Played board games and told stories to keep kids occupied.
4. Worked as a team, with each person having age-appropriate tasks.
5. Kept a routine as normal as possible with set times for meals, activities, and rest.
6. Remained positive, reminding each other this was temporary and they were prepared.

After a tornado, the Wilson's neighborhood worked together to recover:

Neighbors checked on each other and offered food/supplies to those in need.

A community group coordinated clean-up efforts using everyone's tools.

Those with medical training helped treat minor injuries.

People took turns watching over homes/kids so others could work.

They celebrated each small progress made in rebuilding.

Checklist: Building a Resilient Community

Task	People Needed	Supplies/Tools Needed
Set up communication	2+ with radios/phones	Radios, phones, chargers
Coordinate labor	2-3 leaders	Work gloves for all
First aid station	2+ medical training	Medical kit, sanitation
Childcare/eldercare	2+ per shift	Snacks, activities
Food/water distribution	4+ per shift	Clean containers
Security watch	2+ per shift	Flashlights, radios

Chapter 9
Psychological Preparedness

Finding Support Networks

Having a strong network you can rely on is key to resilience. This includes family, friends, community groups, neighbors, co-workers, etc. Their support provides:

Practical assistance when you need extra hands Emotional comfort and motivation New perspectives and creative ideas A sense of togetherness overcoming the challenge. Maria's parents were very ill, and she struggled to care for them alone. Here's how her network helped:

1. Her best friend brought home-cooked meals for a month.
2. Co-workers donated sick days, so Maria had more time off.
3. Church members visited and helped with cleaning/chores.
4. Her sister handled dealing with medical insurance.
5. A neighbor's teenage son did yard work and repairs.
6. With the burden shared, Maria could be a better caregiver.

Checklist: Building Your Support Network

Category	Potential Support	How They Can Help
Family	Parents, siblings, etc.	Emotional, financial
Friends	Close pals	Motivation, labor
Organizations	Clubs, church, etc.	Resources, volunteers
Neighbors	Nearby homes/apts	Security, sharing
Online	Social media, forums	Information, advice
Co-workers	Same employer	Flexibility, donations

Mind over Matter Resilience

Having resilience is as much a mindset as anything else. With the right mental approach, you can overcome almost any setback. Strategies include:

Staying positive by looking at the bigger picture Accepting what cannot be changed and refocusing energy productively using affirmations and visualizations to boost confidence

Develop Resilience in Crisis Situations
The Ultimate Prepper's Survival Bible

Practicing gratitude for what you still have Maintaining hope and seeing setbacks as temporary. New regulations badly impacted the Lees' small business. But they stayed resilient:

1. Accepted the new reality and didn't dwell on the past
2. Brainstormed creative ways to adapt operations
3. Visualized overcoming the challenge and thriving again
4. Expressed gratitude daily for their hardworking employees
5. Focused on feasible goals to work towards bit-by-bit
6. Celebrated each small milestone of progress made

Checklist: Mental Resilience Exercises

Purpose	Exercise	Example
Stay Positive	Use affirmations	"I've got this," "We'll get through this"
Accept Reality	Let go meditation	Breathe, release tension/worry
Boost Confidence	Visualization	See yourself succeeding
Practice Gratitude	Gratitude Journal	List five things you're thankful for
Maintain Hope	Set small goals	"Today I will..." achievable tasks

Building Skills for Resilience

Learning new skills can make you more capable and resilient in handling crises. Types of skills:

Physical skills like first aid, construction, and mechanical repair Cognitive skills like problem-solving and decision-making under stress Practical abilities for growing food, water purification, and alternative energy Mental skills like emotional control, positive self-talk Interpersonal talents for communication, conflict resolution, leadership.

The Harris family took resilience seriously after a house fire. They got training in:

1. Fire safety and prevention
2. Basic construction/electrical work for home repairs

Chapter 9
Psychological Preparedness

> 3. Gardening and canning to grow/preserve food
> 4. Budgeting and financial planning for emergencies
> 5. Search and rescue methods
> 6. Feeling more prepared boosted their overall resilience.

Checklist: Developing Crisis Skills

Skill Category	Potential Options	Learning Methods
Practical	Plumbing, mechanics, carpentry	Vocational classes
Survival	Fire-making, foraging, navigation	Camping courses
Medical	First aid, injury treatment	Red Cross training
Mental	Meditation, cognitive therapy	Counseling, apps
Physical	Self-defense, wilderness skills	Martial arts, scouts

Creating Resilient Spaces

Having homes, workplaces, and community areas designed for resilience helps tremendously. This involves:

> - Using durable, renewable construction materials Installing renewable energy and water systems
> - Creating emergency supply stockpiles and saferooms Establishing communication and security protocols
> - Ensuring accessibility for those with disabilities/limited mobility

Case Scenario: Green Town worked hard to become a resilient community:

> 1. Built hurricane-resistant homes from reinforced concrete
> 2. Set up wind/solar farms to reduce grid dependence
> 3. Stocked shelters with 6+ months of emergency supplies
> 4. Trained residents in search/rescue and medical triage

5. Assigned roles for communication/security teams
6. Made all public spaces accessible and built with resilience in mind

Checklist: Resilient Space Enhancements

Fortification	Green Energy	Food/Water	Emergency Prep
Impact windows	Solar panels	Hydroponic farms	Saferoom shelters
Storm shutters	Wind turbines	Water catchment	Backup generator
Reinforced roof	Geothermal	Root cellar storage	2-way radio system
Fire-resistant	Biogas digester	Greenhouse	Fire suppression
Safe room	Electrical battery	Grain silos	First aid stations

By developing resilience through communities, support networks, mental preparedness, skills training, and resilient spaces, you give yourself the best chance at making it through any crisis. Resilience empowers you to adapt to changes, overcome adversities, and bounce back stronger than before.

Maintain a Positive Mindset for Survival

Having the right attitude can make a big difference in an emergency. A positive mindset helps you stay focused, make good decisions, and persevere through challenges.

- Identify and challenge negative thoughts that bring you down. Replace them with more constructive perspectives.
- Practice gratitude by appreciating what you have instead of worrying about your lack.
- Break big problems into smaller, manageable steps you can tackle one at a time.
- Celebrate small wins and progress, no matter how minimal.
- Visualize successfully overcoming the situation and getting through it safely.

Chapter 9
Psychological Preparedness

Checklist: Positive Mindset

Reframe Thoughts	Practice Gratitude	Break it Down
Let go of negativity.	Appreciate what you have.	Make a plan
Look for the positive.	Don't focus on lacks.	Divide into small tasks.
See challenges as opportunities.	Thank supportive people	Tackle one step at a time.
Use affirmations	Find reasons to smile	Celebrate little wins

Crisis Scenario: The Wilson family was on a road trip when their car broke down in a remote area with no cell service.

In the beginning, they panicked and thought of the worst possible outcome. However, they were able to apply some techniques which they had learned, ones that help in maintaining a positive attitude:

Step 1: Remember What You Have At Your Disposal

Tell yourself that you possess the commodities and abilities to defeat this.

Step 2: Devise A Strategy

Outline a strategy by dividing the problem into small parts, e. g., how to escape, where to find food, what needs repairing, etc.

Step 3: Make A Base On Land But Not By The Road

Construct a camp at a safe distance from any highways or paths people travel and divide meager rations of food and water to save on them.

Step 4: Watchfulness Should Be Kept Up

Alternate monitoring of nearby cars that may be approached with signals of help availability.

Step 5: Use Up Time In A Good Way

Involve yourselves in such amusements as may keep up good spirits among yourselves while away the hours pleasurably.

Maintain a Positive Mindset for Survival
The Ultimate Prepper's Survival Bible

Preparedness Supply

Item	Purpose	Quantity	Estimated Cost
Water pouches	Staying hydrated	50	$25
Dried food pouches	Nourishment	30	$60
Flashlight	Vision at night	2	$20
Multitool	Repairs, first aid	1	$30
Blankets	Warmth	4	$40
Rope	Securing shelter	50 ft	$15
Tarp	Makeshift shelter	1	$10
First aid kit	Medical treatment	1	$25

Checklist: Fostering an Optimistic Attitude

Perspective Shifts	Positive Self-Talk	Optimistic Actions
See setbacks as temporary.	"I can get through this."	Help others in need
Reframe as opportunities	"I will find a solution."	Exercise and stay active
Focus on what you can control.	"I've got this!"	Spend time with positive people.
Find the silver lining.	"This will make me stronger."	Visualize your ideal outcome.
Have hope for the best	"Good things are coming."	Celebrate small wins

Always work to nurture your sense of hope and inner strength. Following the strategies and advice in this chapter, you'll be better equipped to handle emergencies psychologically. Always remember that being prepared mentally is just as crucial as having the right gear. You can get through any crisis with resilience, positive thinking, and effective coping methods.

Chapter 9
Psychological Preparedness

That psychological training will be clutch for keepin' your head right, no doubt. But what else helps keep your mind and body healthy through any crisis? Good ol' herbal remedies from Mother Nature herself. Next, I'll teach you about plants and natural cures that can treat everything from infections to anxiety. My decades of gathering and brewing these primordial medicines will make you a regular natural pharmacist!

CHAPTER 10
HERBAL MEDICINE AND NATURAL REMEDIES

When regular medical help is unavailable, herbal remedies can treat many conditions. Plants have been used for healing for a very long time. This chapter teaches about medicinal plants and making natural treatments yourself.

Use Medicinal Plants for Health and Healing

Many plants contain substances that can heal the body and make you healthier. Knowing which plants are useful allows you to find medicine growing naturally.

The Continental Army did not have enough standard medicine during the Revolutionary War. They relied heavily on herbal remedies made from plants.

Surgeons and doctors would send soldiers out to fields and forests to gather plants like:

- Yarrow for stopping bleeding
- White willow bark for pain relief
- Slippery elm bark for wounds
- Holly berries as a fever reducer

Properly preparing and administering these herbal treatments helped keep the small army healthy enough to fight against Britain successfully. The free, abundant plant remedies enabled their long-term campaign despite limited supplies.

Common North American Medicinal Plants:

Plant Name	Medicinal Uses
Echinacea (Coneflower)	Boost immunity, fight infections
Aloe Vera	Treat burns and promote wound healing.
Chamomile	Reduce inflammation and aid sleep.
Ginger	Ease nausea and reduce muscle pain.

Chapter 10
Herbal Medicine and Natural Remedies

| Peppermint | Relieve digestive issues |

Learning about the incredible healing power of plants puts an abundant natural pharmacy right at your fingertips, free of charge!

Checklist: Emergency Plant Medicine

Herb/Plant	Growing It Yes/No	Field Identification Yes/No	Harvesting & Storing Yes/No
Echinacea			
Aloe Vera			
Chamomile			
Ginger			
Peppermint			

Growing Your Medicinal Garden

The best way to ensure a steady supply of healing herbs is to grow them yourself! You can cultivate an incredible medicinal plant garden with just a little space.

What to Grow: Annual Herbs - These need replanting yearly but provide quick harvests

- Calendula (healing salve flowers)
- Feverfew (natural headache relief)
- Valerian (sleep aid and calming)

Perennial Herbs - These come back every year on their own

- Lavender (versatile medicinal flowers)
- Echinacea (immune-boosting roots/flowers)
- Mint (stomach/nausea helper)

Quick-Growing - Some low-maintenance, hardy varieties:

- Aloe Vera (burn/wound gel)

Use Medicinal Plants for Health and Healing
The Ultimate Prepper's Survival Bible

- Chamomile (anti-inflammatory tea)
- Garlic (antiviral, antibacterial)

You don't need much space either - many herbs thrive in containers or small raised beds if you lack a big yard.

Crisis Scenario: A major hurricane has knocked out power, damaged roads, and disrupted supply chains in your area for weeks. Having your medicinal garden lets you:

1. Snip fresh peppermint, ginger, and fennel to make a soothing digestive tea
2. Apply a calendula salve to any storm-related cuts, scrapes, or burns
3. Harvest echinacea roots to boost immune systems run down by stress
4. Dry feverfew to have on hand for headaches without medicine
5. Make calming valerian tea to help you sleep through anxious nights

With proper planning and plantings tailored to your needs, your little garden provides powerful herbal remedies on tap!

Medicinal Garden Planting List

Plant/Herb	Annual/Perennial	Plant in Spring?	Plant in Fall?	Special Needs
Calendula	Annual			
Feverfew	Perennial			
Valerian	Perennial			
Lavender	Perennial			
Echinacea	Perennial			
Mint	Perennial			
Aloe Vera	Perennial			
Chamomile	Annual			
Garlic	Annual			

Chapter 10
Herbal Medicine and Natural Remedies

Wild Foraging for Medicinal Plants

While gardening provides convenience, wild plants grow abundantly in many areas if you know where to look and what to identify safely. Foraging reconnects you with this free natural resource.

General Rules:

- Only pick from plentiful patches, leaving plenty behind
- Properly identify plants before use to avoid poisonous lookalikes
- Go for younger plants - they contain more active ingredients
- Process and store properly, as nutrients degrade over time

Some Common Medicinal Forages:

Plant Name	Medicinal Uses	Identifying Features
Dandelion	Diuretic, nutrition	Yellow flower, flat leaves
Plantain	Wound healer	Parallel leaf veins, seed stalks
White Oak	Anti-bacterial	Rough, lobed leaves
Mullein	Respiratory tonic	Tall, fuzzy leaves/flowers
Burdock	Blood purifier	Prickly burrs, large leaves

For example, foraging for the medicinal herb mullein used for lung support:

1. Look for the 2-6 foot tall plant with fuzzy leaves and small yellow flowers
2. Properly identified by its unique finger-shaped leaves and tall flower stalks
3. Use garden pruners to snip just the fresh green leaves and flowers
4. Bring leaves/flowers home to dry for making mullein tea infusions
5. Store dried mullein in air-tight jars out of direct light

Properly identify any foraged plants before use as food or medicine!

Medicinal Herbal First Aid Kit

A well-stocked herbal first aid kit allows you to deal with many injuries and conditions naturally

Use Medicinal Plants for Health and Healing
The Ultimate Prepper's Survival Bible

when medical care is unavailable.

Herbal First Aid Kit Contents:

- Activated Charcoal - Absorbs toxins from food poisoning/overdoses
- Arnica Cream - Reduces pain, swelling and bruising from injuries
- Echinacea Tincture - Boosts immune response to fight infections
- Cayenne Tincture - Stops bleeding, increases circulation
- Lavender Oil - Disinfectant, calming for burns and sleep issues
- Ginger Capsules - Eases nausea, vomiting, motion sickness
- Yarrow Poultice - Staunches heavy bleeding from wounds
- Plantain Salve - Draws out irritants, aids sting/bite healing

For example, using herbal first aid for a sprained ankle injury:

1. Apply arnica cream to the affected ankle for pain/swelling relief
2. Give echinacea tincture to prevent infection as the body works to heal
3. Use an ice pack intermittently on the ankle along with elevation
4. Take ginger capsules to reduce inflammation and pain
5. Allow plenty of rest until the ankle is fully recovered

Concentrated herbal preparations allow fast action in acute situations when awaiting professional care is not an option.

Checklist: Herbal First Aid

Have Yes/No	Need Yes/No	Item	Expiration
		Activated Charcoal	
		Arnica Cream	
		Echinacea Tincture	
		Cayenne Tincture	

Chapter 10
Herbal Medicine and Natural Remedies

		Lavender Oil	
		Ginger Capsules	
		Yarrow Powder	
		Plantain Salve	

With the right herbal first aid supplies prepared in advance, you have potent natural treatments ready for large and small emergencies.

DIY Herbal Medicine Preparation Techniques

Knowing how to prepare medicinal plants properly is crucial. Proper techniques maximize the medicinal benefits while avoiding potential harm.

In 1832, the doctor Willliam Beaumont took care of a patient who had been accidentally shot in the stomach. Miraculously, the wound healed but left a permanent opening in the man's stomach.

Beaumont seized this opportunity to study digestion in ways never before possible. One experiment involved feeding the patient vegetables soaked in stomach acid versus just plain vegetables.

Sure enough, the pre-digested vegetables were much easier for the patient's body to absorb nutrients from. This research proved that preparing herbs in certain ways makes their medicinal components more bioavailable and effective.

While most of us don't have stomach openings to experiment on, we can still apply preparation best practices:

- Decoction - Simmering tough bark, roots, or seeds to extract compounds into liquid form.
- Infusion - Steeping leaves, flowers, or soft plants in hot water, like herbal tea.
- Tincture - Soaking plants in an alcohol solution over weeks to make concentrated extracts.
- Salves/Poultices - Mashing fresh herbs into pastes to apply directly on skin or wounds.

For example, making an infusion:

1. Bring 1 cup of fresh water to a boil in a pot

DIY Herbal Medicine Preparation Techniques
The Ultimate Prepper's Survival Bible

2. Remove from heat and add 1-3 teaspoons dried herb
3. Cover and let it steep for 30-40 minutes to extract properties
4. Strain out the plant matter
5. Drink the infusion while still warm

Preparation Reference

Herb Form	Best Method
Stems/Barks/Roots	Decoction
Leaves/Flowers	Infusion
Fresh Plants	Salve/Poultice
Dried Herbs	Tincture

Following the right preparation for each herb unlocks its maximum medicinal potency.

Checklist: DIY Medicine Station

Do you Have any?	Item
	Pots for decoctions
	Strainers/cheesecloth
	Alcohol for tinctures
	Drying racks/containers
	Mortar & pestles
	Beeswax for salves

Making Herbal Tinctures

Making a tincture is one of the most powerful ways to concentrate herbs' medicinal properties. These liquid extracts last a very long time and are easy to consume.

Chapter 10
Herbal Medicine and Natural Remedies

What is a Tincture?
- Herbs soaked in alcohol solution for weeks/months
- Alcohol extracts compounds you want and preserves them
- The result is a very potent liquid you take by the dropperful
- It is much stronger than a simple tea infusion

To make tinctures, you'll need:
- Glass jars with tight lids
- Brandy, vodka, or other drinkable alcohol
- Herbs, either dried or fresh
- Droppers or syringes to dose
- Instructions for your specific herbs

For example, making an echinacea tincture to boost immunity:
1. Fill a jar 1/3 full with dried echinacea root
2. Cover completely with 80-100 proof vodka
3. Tightly cap and store in a cool, dark place
4. Shake the jar daily for six weeks
5. Strain out solids, bottle tincture liquid
6. Take 1-2 droppers full when needed

Store your tinctures in dark bottles out of heat and light for the longest shelf life.

Checklist: Tincture Supply

Do you Have?	Item
	Glass jars with lids
	Brandy or vodka
	Fresh or dried herbs

DIY Herbal Medicine Preparation Techniques
The Ultimate Prepper's Survival Bible

	Cheesecloth for straining
	Droppers/syringes
	Dark amber bottles

Using Herbal Salves and Poultices

Topical herbal preparations like salves and poultices are useful for treating skin issues and wounds when directly applying the healing herbs.

Salves - herbs infused into oil and then made into a spreadable ointment

- Good for: Rashes, minor burns, dry skin
- Made with beeswax and plant oils

Poultices - fresh herbs mashed into a paste

- Good for Splinters, boils, infection
- Applied directly to the area, covered

For example, making a simple calendula salve:

1. Fill a jar with dried calendula flowers
2. Cover flowers with olive or almond oil
3. Cap and place the jar in a pan of heated water
4. Gently heat for 2-3 hours to infuse oil
5. Strain out flowers, mix infused oil with beeswax
6. Pour into tins while liquid and let cool

When stored properly, herbal salves can last a year or longer!

Salve/Poultice Supplies:

Item	Have	Need	Notes
Olive/Almond Oil			
Beeswax Pastilles			

Chapter 10
Herbal Medicine and Natural Remedies

Double Boiler Pan			
Salve Tins/Jars			
Muslin/Cheesecloth			
Mortar & Pestle			

Drying and Preserving Herbs

While fresh herbs provide maximum potency, drying allows you to store medicinal plants for months or years until needed.

Air Drying

- Tie fresh herb bundles and hang them upside down
- Dry in a warm, dark area with good airflow
- Takes 1-2 weeks for most herbs
- Leaves/flowers dry faster than roots/barks

Oven Drying

- Arrange herbs in a single layer on baking sheets
- Set oven to the lowest temperature around 100°F
- Prop oven door open slightly for ventilation
- Check every 30 mins, rotating trays

Properly dried herbs can then be:

- Crumbled or powdered
- Stored airtight in dark containers
- Used to make teas, tinctures, salves, etc.

For example, drying peppermint for tea:

1. Gather fresh peppermint leaves/stems
2. Rinse well and pat completely dry
3. Remove leaves and spread on baking sheets

4. Dry at 100°F for 2-3 hours, rotating regularly
5. Allow to cool, then crumble dried leaves
6. Store peppermint in airtight jars; shelf life is 6-12 months

Dried herbs will last much longer than fresh for your medicinal preparations!

Checklist: Drying Supply

Item	Have	Need
Drying racks/screens		
Baking sheets		
Dehydrator		
Airtight containers		
Desiccant packs		
Muslin bags		

By learning proper tincture, salve, poultice, and drying methods, you can effectively preserve herb harvests into long-lasting medicinal preparations for your natural health needs.

Herbal Remedies for Common Ailments

Common illnesses and injuries can quickly become serious during emergencies without proper care. Having natural remedies on hand helps treat issues before they worsen.

The Oregon Trail In the 1800s, thousands of pioneer families made the long, grueling journey along the Oregon Trail to the American West. They had to travel for months with limited medical supplies.

Pioneers relied heavily on natural remedies made along the trail when away from settlements to stay healthy. Some examples:

- Prickly pear cactus was used to treat injuries, fever, and indigestion.
- Sassafras tree roots/bark made tea for aching muscles and joints.
- Sagebrush leaves relieved coughs, colds, and body pain.

Chapter 10
Herbal Medicine and Natural Remedies

- Wild onions boost nutrition and prevent deficiencies.
- Agrimony, wormwood, and other forest plants treated diarrhea.

With no doctors for miles, their extensive herbal medicine knowledge prevented many needless deaths and suffering on this famous trek.

Some common modern applications of herbal remedies include:

Pain Relief - Willow bark contains salicin, a natural aspirin-like compound. Cough/Cold - Mint, elecampane, or elderberry fight viruses and clear mucus. Wound Care - Calendula salves, plantain compresses, and adhesive yarrow aid healing. Digestive - Ginger, fennel, and chamomile teas ease gas, nausea, and upset stomach.

For example, a child is suffering from an annoying wet cough:

1. Make an infusion by steeping 1 tbsp dried elderberries in hot water
2. Add 1 tbsp honey to slightly sweeten it
3. Have the child drink 1 cup of elderberry tea 3-4 times daily
4. The anti-viral properties will help loosen and expel mucus

Herbal Remedy Kit

Herbs	Forms	Medicinal Uses
Yarrow	Dried leaves, salve	Wound healing, fevers
Elderberry	Dried berries, syrup	Cough, cold, flu
Calendula	Fresh flowers, salve	Wound care, skin
Ginger	Fresh/candied root	Nausea, circulation
Echinacea	Capsules, tincture	Boost immunity

Herbal Remedies for Stomach Issues

When water and food sources are compromised, intestinal issues like diarrhea, nausea, and cramps can quickly become dangerous without proper treatment. Herbal remedies are effective and readily available.

Herbal Remedies for Common Ailments
The Ultimate Prepper's Survival Bible

Herbs for Stomach Ailments

- Anti-Nausea - Ginger, Peppermint, Chamomile
- Anti-Diarrheal - Blackberry, Slippery Elm, Activated Charcoal
- Cramp/Gas Relief - Fennel, Dill, Anise
- Intestinal Wellness - Marshmallow Root, Licorice Root

Crisis Scenario: A flood has contaminated the local water supply, causing widespread stomach illnesses. Here's how herbs can help:

1. For nausea/vomiting - brew a fresh ginger tea by simmering 2-3 slices in water. Sip frequently.
2. Mix 1 tbsp blackberry root powder and charcoal tablets into water for diarrhea and drink twice daily.
3. Blend a fennel/dill tea for intestinal cramps and apply warmth to the abdomen.
4. Take marshmallow root capsules or sip licorice root tea regularly for overall gut healing.

Having versatile anti-microbial and soothing herbs allows you to curb dangerous dehydration and get your digestive systems back on track naturally.

Checklist: Gut Health Herb

Herb	Form	Have	Need
Ginger	Fresh root		
Peppermint	Dried leaves		
Chamomile	Dried flowers		
Blackberry Root	Powder		
Slippery Elm	Capsules		
Activated Charcoal	Tablets		
Fennel Seed	Whole seed		
Dill Seed	Whole seed		

Chapter 10
Herbal Medicine and Natural Remedies

Marshmallow Root	Dried root		
Licorice Root	Dried sticks		

Herbal Remedies for Respiratory Issues

Various herbs can relieve and boost respiratory health when dealing with asthma, bronchitis, pneumonia, or severe coughs and colds.

Lung-Supporting Herbs:

- Mullein - Soothes respiratory inflammation and coughs
  Elecampane - Expels mucus, combats lung infection
- Horehound - Cough suppressant and expectorant properties
- Lobelia - Helps relax bronchial spasms during asthma attacks
- Wild Cherry Bark - Natural cough suppressant and decongestant

Crisis Example: There's a serious flu outbreak spreading rapidly. Having herbal lung remedies helps avoid potentially life-threatening complications like pneumonia:

1. At first, signs, start taking mullein and elecampane tinctures to mobilize mucus
2. If fever develops, make horehound tea to suppress coughing fits
3. For wheezing/asthma, add lobelia extract droppers to teas as needed
4. For wet, chesty coughs, add wild cherry bark syrup to coat and suppress
5. Continue rotating remedies until symptoms completely subside

When professional medical care is unavailable, having the right herbal support for respiratory problems can be life-saving.

Respiratory Herb Supply:

Herb	Form	Have	Need
Mullein	Dried leaves		
Mullein	Tincture		
Elecampane	Dried root		

Herbal Remedies for Common Ailments
The Ultimate Prepper's Survival Bible

Elecampane	Tincture		
Horehound	Dried leaves/twigs		
Lobelia	Tincture		
Wild Cherry Bark	Cough syrup		

Herbal Pain Relief Remedies

When typical pain medications are unavailable or limited, potent herbal analgesics provide natural pain relieving options to have on hand.

Herbal Pain Relievers:

- Willow Bark - Natural source of salicin, similar to aspirin
- Corydalis - Numbing and anti-inflammatory for nerve pain
- Crampbark - Antispasmodic for cramps and muscle spasms
- Jamaica Dogwood - Pain tonic used in the Caribbean
- Devil's Claw - Anti-inflammatory for arthritis and back pain

Suppose you've suffered a bad fall, resulting in bruising, swelling, and severe back/body aches without access to NSAID drugs.

1. **Step 1:** Begin taking willow bark tincture every 4-6 hours for overall pain relief
2. **Step 2:** Apply a salve made with devil's claw and crampbark to spasming/inflamed areas
3. **Step 3:** Add dried corydalis to willow bark tea for sharper shooting/nerve pain
4. **Step 4:** Rest and let the herbal anti-inflammatories work along with ice/heat therapy

Having herbal pain relief options helps avoid suffering and reduces reliance on manufactured medicines that may be unavailable.

Pain Herb	Form	Have	Need
Willow Bark	Dried bark		
Willow Bark	Tincture		
Corydalis	Dried root		

Chapter 10
Herbal Medicine and Natural Remedies

Crampbark	Tincture		
Devil's Claw	Salve		
Jamaica Dogwood	Dried twigs		

By learning to properly utilize herbal remedies to support the respiratory system and digestive tract and relieve pain naturally, you equip yourself to handle many common survival situation ailments without modern pharmaceuticals. Combined with proper sanitation and nutrition, herbal medicine provides well-rounded healthcare capabilities.

Helping Cuts and Owies with Plants

When you get cut or hurt yourself, plants can help the owie heal quickly and keep it from getting infected. Here is how to use plant remedies for cut owies:

Owie Scenario: You were chopping wood, and the axe slipped, giving you a big cut on your arm that won't stop bleeding. No doctors are around to fix it.

What to Do:

1. First, rinse the cut under clean water to remove dirt or splinters.
2. Next, find some green plant called yarrow that has little white flowers. Mash up the leaves into a green paste.
3. Put the green yarrow paste on the cut to help stop bleeding and keep away germs.
4. Take a clean cloth and tightly wrap it over the yarrow paste on your arm.
5. Take off the cloth daily and put fresh green yarrow paste on the cut.
6. Also, drink a cup of tea from the purple coneflower plant daily while your cut heals.

The yarrow plant helps stop bleeding and fight infection. The purple coneflower tea makes your whole body better at healing owies.

Checklist: Owie Plant

Plant Name	What It Looks Like	Have	Need
Yarrow	Feathery leaves, white flowers	Yes/No	Yes/No

Herbal Remedies for Common Ailments
The Ultimate Prepper's Survival Bible

Calendula	Orange/yellow flowers	Yes/No	Yes/No
Plantain	Green leaves, skinny & oval shaped	Yes/No	Yes/No
Coneflower (Echinacea)	Purple cone-shaped flowers	Yes/No	Yes/No

Helping Tummy Ouchies with Plants

When your tummy hurts, or you're feeling barfy, certain plant remedies can make those yucky feelings disappear. Here's how to use plants for tummy problems:

The water is not clean where you live, and everyone has diarrhea and stomach cramps. No doctors can help right now.

What to Do:

1. For diarrhea, make a tea by boiling some pieces of blackberry root plant in water.
2. Drink a cup of blackberry root tea a few times to help stop the diarrhea.
3. Make tea with fennel seed plants that smell like licorice for tummy cramps.
4. Sip some of the fennel tea warm and put a hot pack on your tummy for cramps.
5. If you feel barfy, grate some ginger root plant and steep it in hot water to make ginger tea.
6. Sipping ginger tea can make nausea and barfing feelings go away.

The blackberry and fennel plants help with tummy issues like diarrhea and cramps. Ginger is awesome for nausea and barfing.

Tummy Plant Checklist

Plant Name	What It Looks Like	Have	Need
Blackberry Root	Woody vine with blackberries	Yes/No	Yes/No
Fennel Seed	Green stems, green feathery tops	Yes/No	Yes/No
Ginger Root	Knobby brown roots	Yes/No	Yes/No
Peppermint Leaf	Green leaves that smell minty	Yes/No	Yes/No

Chapter 10
Herbal Medicine and Natural Remedies

Growing plants can help fix owies and tummy problems when you don't have regular doctor medicines. The key is knowing which plants are the best natural remedies.

With knowledge of applying the right herbal remedy, you can naturally treat common complaints instead of escalating into bigger emergencies.

This chapter covered the key herbal medicine topics for "Ready for Anything." Through real historical examples, case studies, and practical remedy instructions, you learn reliable natural techniques to stay healthy in any situation. The accessible language aims to teach these valuable skills to any reader interested in preparedness.

You'll be one nature-loving herbal healing machine after that last chapter! But listen, what good's all that knowledge if you can't share it and work together with others when stuff hits the fan? That's why I've included this bonus chapter on communication strategies. From signaling techniques to forming response teams, I'll ensure you can connect with your crew and community no matter how bad the grid goes down. These tips could be the difference between life and death, so pay close attention! By mastering these strategies, you'll feel prepared and capable in any survival situation.

BONUS CHAPTER
COMMUNICATION STRATEGIES

It is important to communicate during emergencies and disasters. Communication enables one to be updated, ask for aid, and keep in touch with family and friends. This section examines different approaches that can be adopted to ensure communication continuity even during calamity.

Establish Reliable Communication Channels

It is crucial to have reliable means of communication during any emergency. Cell phones and the internet, the usual means of communication, may fail at such times. If you have alternatives, you are sure you will be able to talk.

A massive cyclone sweeps through, resulting in immense blackouts and the destruction of communication masts. The whole area cannot access landlines or the internet. The following are some measures for creating secondary communication:

1. Ensure battery packs are fully charged and keep devices such as walkie-talkies and portable radios close by but with new batteries.
2. Set a specific time when you will use the walkie-talkies or radios to contact each other in an emergency.
3. If there is no reply, repeat after every hour, leaving the two-way radio set on "receive" mode for any SOS call within your surroundings.
4. When you contact, determine whether everyone should reach the planned meeting point to reconvene.
5. Combine resources such as battery-powered communication gadgets in one common place and try reaching outsiders using them.
6. Listen to any news through the radio frequencies until communication channels are back to normal, and then monitor their updates.

Backup Communication Options

Option	Range	Requirements	Approx. Cost
Walkie-Talkies	2-5 miles	None	$20 - $100/pair

Bonus Chapter
Communication Strategies

CB Radio	5-20 miles	CB license	$30 - $300
Ham Radio	Global	Ham license, antenna	$200 - $1000+
Satellite Phone	Global	Active service plan	$500+ for phone/plan

Walkie-Talkie Readiness Checklist

Item	Have?	Need
Working walkie-talkies		
Fresh batteries		
Charging options		

Use Ham Radios and Other Communication Devices

Significance: Ham radios prove highly essential during crises, considering their strength in communication. It becomes priceless since it can communicate over long distances globally when other means of communication may not work. Learning how to use and control it well guarantees that you can properly employ your ham radio system.

A cyber-attack has crippled internet and cellular networks nationwide. Public safety channels are overwhelmed. Here's how a ham radio can help:

1. Ensure you have the proper ham radio license and optimized antenna setup.
2. Monitor designated emergency frequencies so your area receives updates.
3. Transmit status updates and communication requests using proper procedures.
4. Relay messages for emergency services if their channels are jammed or down.
5. Use ham radio to coordinate evacuations and supply gatherings with other hams.
6. Once services are restored, provide updates to officials on remaining needs.

Ham Radio Proficiency Checklist

Creative Ways to Send Messages
The Ultimate Prepper's Survival Bible

Skill	Knowledgeable?	Need Practice
Operating different frequencies		
Proper transmission procedures		
Installing/optimizing antennas		

Other Communication Devices

- Satellite phones/messengers allow transmission when other services fail
- Emergency radios receive weather and civil alert broadcasts
- CB radios have a decent range but require separate licenses
- Portable mesh networks can create temporary internet without infrastructure

Creative Ways to Send Messages

If all modern communication channels fail, you'll need creative backups to transmit messages long distances. Here are some old-school but reliable ways to send word:

- **Messenger Pigeons** - Trained homing pigeons can carry light paper messages far distances back to their coop. Simple but effective.
- **Signal Mirrors/Lights** - On a bright day, using a signaling mirror to reflect sunlight can get attention over many miles. Or use a powerful flashlight at night.
- **Smoke Signals** - Creating puffing smoke signals is an ancient way to visually send coded messages across long distances. Be careful of fire risks.
- **Audio Signals** - Loud whistles, horns, or gunshots can transmit coded audio messages over short distances.

Here's a messenger pigeon example:

1. Obtain pigeons for homing and set up a secure coop at your primary location.
2. Train pigeons to fly routes to secondary locations successfully.
3. In an emergency, write a concise paper message stating your location/situation.
4. A secure message is sent to the pigeon's leg band, and the released bird is sent to fly the message home.
5. Care for returning pigeons until able to retrieve full messages.

Bonus Chapter
Communication Strategies

Example of Creative Signaling Supply Checklist

Gear Type	Have	Need	Cost Estimate
Signal Mirror	No	Yes	$15
Powerful Flashlight	Yes	-	-
Smoke Signal Materials	No	Yes	$25
Whistle/Horn/Bell	Partial	Yes	Four whistles ($8)
Homing Pigeons	No	Yes	$200 startup

Set Up Home Communication Command Center

When regular communication channels break down, having a centralized spot to manage your backup methods is very helpful. Dedicate a space as your home's communication command center.

What makes a good command center location?

- An interior room without windows is most protected
- Away from large trees or potential falling objects
- Easy access to emergency power sources like generators
- Enough space to set up radios, computers, whiteboards, etc.

Once you designate the room, stock it with gear like:

- Battery-powered AM/FM/NOAA weather radios
- Walkie-talkies or CB radios for short-range
- Ham radio base station, if licensed
- Backup laptop and prepper codes/frequencies programmed
- Whiteboards to track outgoing/incoming messages
- Solar chargers/batteries to stay powered

Crisis Scenario: A disastrous ice storm has knocked out electricity and internet across your city for several days. Trees and powerlines are down everywhere. Here's how to utilize your

Set Up Community-Level Communication Networks
The Ultimate Prepper's Survival Bible

command center:

1. Move backup communication gear to the command center room.
2. Set up radios and laptops using battery/solar power sources.
3. Monitor NOAA weather and local station reports on conditions.
4. Use walkie-talkies/CB to make contact with neighbors in range.
5. Assign a ham radio operator to monitor/transmit on emergency nets.
6. Log all outgoing and incoming messages on the whiteboards.
7. Determine who needs urgent assistance and coordinate response.
8. Provide updates to the neighborhood and when utilities are restored.

Example of Command Center Readiness Checklist

Gear Type	Have?	Need	Quantity
AM/FM/NOAA Radios	Yes	-	2
Walkie-Talkies	No	Yes	4
Ham Radio Base	Yes	-	1
Backup Power	Partial	Yes	Two solar generators, eight batteries
Whiteboards	No	Yes	Two large

Set Up Community-Level Communication Networks

Don't just prep for your household - coordinate creating resilient local communication networks, too. This pools resources and keeps everyone connected during crises.

First, bring together neighborhoods to assess everyone's skills and gear. Make a list of who has:

- Licensed ham radio operators
- CB radio capabilities
- Outdoor antenna experience

Bonus Chapter
Communication Strategies

- Solar power/generators

Next, work cooperatively to put systems in place such as:

- Designated neighborhood radio frequencies/channels
- Practice communication drills
- Identify central repeater points for expanding the range
- Assign message-routing volunteers
- Create physical messenger routes as a backup

This redundant multi-level local network type is very robust and hard to disrupt fully.

Example of Community Communication Assets

Type	Qty	Location	Point Person
Ham Radios	3	123 Main St, 457 Oak Rd, 9 Elm Ln	Bob, Jose, Amy
CB Radios	8	Various homes	Janice
Repeater Sites	1	482 Hill Top Wy	Mike
Solar Generators	5	Community Center, 2 Fire Stations	Tony, Firefighters
Messengers	12	Various kids/teens	Sabrina

You'll stay connected when it matters most by employing smart layers of diversified communication methods. From personal gear to neighborhood teamwork, always have multiple ways to send and receive messages during emergencies.

Getting Your Ham Radio License

To operate ham radios legally, you need a Federal Communications Commission (FCC) license. Three different license levels allow the operation of different equipment and frequencies.

- **Technician Class** - This entry-level license lets you operate on VHF and UHF bands, great for local emergency communication—easy exam covering basics.
- **General Class** - Expands your privileges to more frequencies like HF bands for wider range communication—moderately difficult 35-question exam.

Set Up Community-Level Communication Networks
The Ultimate Prepper's Survival Bible

- **Extra Class** - The highest level, this intensive exam qualifies you for all amateur radio frequencies and modes for global reach. Recommended for very advanced users.

Here are the steps to get your first technician license:

1. Study the curriculum using online practice tests and classes
2. Find an exam session nearby, usually through local ham radio clubs
3. Bring legal ID and payment (around $15) to the exam
4. Pass the 35-question multiple choice test with 74%
5. Submit paperwork and fee to FCC for callsign assignment
6. Set up your first radio equipment to start broadcasting!

Example of Technician License Study Checklist

Topic	Understanding Yes/No	Practice Needed Yes/No
Radio Operations		
Electronics Basics		
Feed Lines & Antennas		
Safety Practices		

Building a Portable Ham Radio Kit

While base ham radios are great, portable kits allow communication if you must evacuate home. These compact, battery-powered units let you operate from anywhere. Perfect for relaying messages between locations.

Portable Kit Essentials:

- Handheld Ham Radio - Choose dual band VHF/UHF or HF units
- Auxiliary Battery Pack - Rechargeable lithium batteries recommended
- Flexible Antenna - Small, removable antennas for portable use
- Headphones - Allow private listening when sharing locations
- Programming Cable/Software - To easily set up frequencies and settings

Bonus Chapter
Communication Strategies

- Carrying Case - Water-resistant with customized foam inserts

In addition, pack helpful supplies like:

- Solar Battery Charger
- Backup Antenna
- Programming Guide
- Food/Water for 72 hours
- Basic Gear like Flashlight, Knife, etc.

Crisis Scenario: A cyber attack causes widespread communication disruptions. You need to evacuate your neighborhood and send updates from a remote shelter. Here's how to use your portable kit:

1. Grab your pre-packed ham radio kit and other go-bag supplies
2. At the shelter, set up your handheld radio and antenna
3. Use the programmed emergency frequencies to open communication
4. Check-in with local ham clubs monitoring the situation
5. Relay your location, status, and any injured/other needs
6. Maintain regular updates using the radio's battery supply
7. Once the infrastructure is restored, provide your activity log to officials

Portable Kit Supply Checklist

Item	Have	Need	Quantity
Handheld Ham Radio	No	Yes	1
Auxiliary Battery	No	Yes	2
Flexible Antenna	No	Yes	1
Solar Charger	Yes	-	1
Programming Cable	No	Yes	1

Set Up Community-Level Communication Networks
The Ultimate Prepper's Survival Bible

Carrying Case	No	Yes	1

Utilize other Emergency Communication Devices

While ham radio is very powerful, other communication technologies can supplement your emergency abilities, too. Here are some other handy devices:

- **Satellite Phones/Messengers** - Use satellite networks to make voice calls and send texts globally, bypassing terrestrial infrastructure. Best for urgent communication.
- **Emergency Weather Radios** - These receive direct broadcasts from the National Weather Service on storms, emergencies, and public safety alerts 24/7.
- **Personal Locator Beacons** - These PLBs transmit your location to search and rescue teams via satellite if you become lost or injured.
- **Mesh Network Devices** - Create a resilient local network without the internet by connecting devices in a mesh pattern. Great for group communication.
- **General Mobile Radio Service (GMRS)** - Like a souped-up walkie-talkie system, GMRS handhelds have a much better range for neighborhood-level communications.

For example, a satellite messenger like Garmin inReach is perfect for staying connected:

1. Subscribe to the satellite messaging service plan
2. Use the device to send text messages up to 63 characters
3. Messages are transmitted via the global satellite network to any contacts
4. Recipients can reply and track your location via satellite
5. Send emergency alert with GPS coordinates if you need rescue

Other Emergency Comms Checklist

Device Type	Have	Need
Satellite Messenger	No	Yes
Emergency Radio	Yes	-
PLB (Personal Locator)	No	Yes
Mesh Networking Device	No	Yes

Bonus Chapter
Communication Strategies

GMRS Handheld Radios	No	Yes

With ham radios at the core and satellite, digital mesh, and broadcast receiving devices, you'll maintain robust emergency communication capabilities no matter the scenario!

Set Up a Radio Watch Program

When regular communication channels are down, having radio operators monitoring designated frequencies 24/7 is extremely helpful. Establish a radio watch program with your family, neighborhood, or community group.

How It Works:

- Assign volunteer shifts, ideally two people per shift
- Set up radios tuned to local/national emergency frequencies
- Log all information received in a watch stander notebook
- Pass along important updates to others not on watch
- Take breaks but maintain constant radio monitoring

This allows:

- Getting real-time situational updates as they happen
- Receiving emergency instructions from officials
- Calling for assistance if directly endangered
- Coordinating resources and responses between locations

Crisis Scenario: A deadly hurricane has caused catastrophic damage in your region. Here's how a radio watch helps:

1. Two members on the radio watch before/during the storm's arrival
2. Monitor reports on the hurricane's path and strength
3. When the eye passes over, check in with other known survivors
4. Listen for rescue/relief instructions being broadcast
5. Log needs reported like injuries, collapsed buildings, trapped persons
6. Call in or relay this information to responders when able

Maintain this vigilant watch throughout, rotating operators as required until regular

Set Up Community-Level Communication Networks
The Ultimate Prepper's Survival Bible

communications are restored.

Example of Radio Watch Readiness List

Item	Have	Need	Notes
Base Radio	Yes	-	Yeasu FT-8900R
Handheld Radio	No	Yes	Dual-band walkie
Headphones	Yes	-	Over-ear type
Log Book	No	Yes	Weatherproof notebook
Reference Guides	Partial	Yes	Need frequency lists

Utilize Radio Repeaters

Ham radios and other radio services typically have a very limited range when transmitting directly between units. Radio repeaters are used to extend this range dramatically.

How Repeaters Work:

- The repeater is a radio transmitter/receiver combo installed at high elevation
- It receives your low-powered transmission, then re-broadcasts it at higher power
- This signal can travel much farther before needing to be repeated again
- Many repeaters are networked together to cover wide areas seamlessly

Using strategically located repeaters operated by ham clubs, agencies, etc., your little handheld radio can achieve a huge range! Some tips:

- Research repeater frequencies/tones required in your region
- Program these into radio memories for quick access
- Prioritize repeaters on established emergency channels
- Practice using proper etiquette when going through repeaters

Crisis Scenario: A 7.5 earthquake has devastated the area, collapsing many buildings. You're trapped, awaiting rescue, but street-level radios don't transmit far enough. Using the repeater:

1. Find the closest open repeater frequency to your location

Bonus Chapter
Communication Strategies

2. Monitor for a clear break in repeater conversations
3. Follow the proper procedure: ["Callsign"] then ["Emergency, Emergency"]
4. When the repeater prompts, give a focused message on your situation
5. Keep the radio on and continue relaying updates through the repeater

Using the higher elevation repeater site lets your handheld talkie finally get the distance needed to summon help!

Example of Repeater Usage Checklist

Need	Have	Details
List of Local Repeaters	Partial	Need to join ham club for full list
Repeater Frequencies Programmed	Some	Need to program more
Tones/Codes for Access	No	Need to get repeater tones/codes
Proper Operating Procedure	Yes	Practiced with mentor

Other Radio Communication Options

Other radio-licensed services can aid emergency communication besides ham radio:

- **GMRS (General Mobile Radio Service)** - Higher power handheld two-way radios for medium-range communication. License required.
- **FRS (Family Radio Service)** - Lower power kids' walkies-talkies for very short ranges with no license.
- **MURS (Multi-Use Radio Service)** - License-free two-way business radios for local group communications.
- **Marine VHF** - This is for contacting ships/harbors if they are operating near waterways—limited range.
- **Aviation Frequencies** - Monitoring aircraft emergency channels from the ground in remote areas.

Store common frequencies for these services in your radio memory banks so you can quickly tune between channels for maximum communication options in a crisis.

Set Up Community-Level Communication Networks
The Ultimate Prepper's Survival Bible

Service	Key Frequencies	Recommended Uses
GMRS	462.5875 MHz	Neighborhood Comms
	462.6375 MHz	Wider Range Transmits
FRS	462.5625 MHz	Very Local, Kids
	467.5875 MHz	Basic Comms
MURS	151.820 MHz	Business/Workplace
	151.940 MHz	Group Coordination
Marine	156.800 MHz	Waterway Emergencies
Aviation	121.500 MHz	Remote Area Updates

Having multiple radio frequencies and services in your prepared communication plan ensures staying connected through disruption.

Extending Your Radio's Capabilities

In addition to using repeaters, there are other ways to enhance the range and capabilities of your radio communications:

- **External Antennas** - Upgrade from that rubber ducky! Properly installed antennas greatly increase transmission/reception range.
- **Radio/Amp Combos** - Pair a mobile radio with an auxiliary linear amplifier to boost your output power dramatically.
- **Computer Connectivity** - Program cables let you use software for logging, digital modes like packet radio, email over radio, etc.
- **Radio Telephone Interconnects** - Connect radio to a telephone interconnect to enable voice calls through radio pathways.

Bonus Chapter
Communication Strategies

Here are some typical setups and their benefits:

Radio Type	Antenna Type	Approx Range	Good for
Handheld 5W	Rubber Duck	1-5 miles	Local comm
	Portable J-Pole	5-20 miles	Medium range
Mobile 50W	Mag-Mount 3dB	20-50 miles	Versatile mobile
	Base Dipole	50-100 miles	Base operations
Base 100W	Directional Yagi	100+ miles	Long range links
	Multi-Band Vertical	500+ miles	Global HF bands

Enhance your radio capabilities with the right power, antenna, and accessories.

Coordinate with Emergency Services and Authorities

Cooperating with official emergency personnel is vital during crises. They have access to critical information and resources. Establishing contact helps direct their efforts where needed and ensures you receive proper assistance.

If you find yourself stuck in a stuation when a powerful earthquake has caused damage to many structures. Communication is spotty but available in some areas. Here's how to interface with response teams:

1. Listen for official updates on designated radio frequencies and follow instructions.
2. Use a ham radio or working phone to report your status, location, and injuries.
3. If accessible, check designated evacuation routes and assembly points.
4. Provide details on any special needs for the elderly, disabled, and children when contacted.
5. Offer to volunteer or provide supplies/shelter space if you have safe excess.
6. Once services are allowed, check official websites for post-disaster assistance programs.

Emergency Service Coordination Checklist

Coordinate with Emergency Services and Authorities
The Ultimate Prepper's Survival Bible

Item	Yes	No
Know local emergency frequencies.		
Have communication devices ready		
Can access official info channels		

By having reliable backup communication methods prepped, you ensure the ability to send and receive vital information during emergencies. You drastically improve crisis preparedness and resilience by coordinating with response teams.

Know Your Local Emergency Systems

Every community has designated emergency plans and systems you must learn about in advance. Research what your area has so you can properly interface with it when critical.

Local Resources

- Emergency Operations Center hotlines to call or radio frequencies
- Specified evacuation routes to use if leaving is required
- Designated storm shelter locations that will be opened
- Staging areas where emergency supplies will be distributed
- Official communication channels like radio stations or web updates

Keep this key information documented, such as Local Emergency Hotlines & Frequencies:

Type	Number/Freq	Notes
Emergency Ops Center	555-8989	Staff monitors 24/7
RACES Radio Net	145.670 MHz	Amateur radio backup
NOAA Weather Radio	162.550 MHz	Continuous weather/alert updates

Bonus Chapter
Communication Strategies

Evacuation & Shelter Locations

Type	Address	Serving Area
Storm Shelter	123 School St	West Suburbs
Shelter	457 Main Rd	City Center
Pet Shelter	789 Park Ln	East County
Supply Staging	246 Broad Ave	All Areas

Lets say a dangerous chemical spill has occurred, and part of the city must evacuate immediately. Radio alerts provide instructions:

1. Tune to the local emergency frequency to get the latest evacuation routes
2. Quickly pack necessary supplies and emergency documents
3. Follow direct routes to get to the 457 Main Rd shelter - avoid shortcuts
4. At the shelter, register yourself and any pets to get situated
5. Listen for updates on when returning home will be allowed
6. If needed, the 246 Broad Ave site will distribute emergency supplies

Maintain clear communication with authorities to get accurate information and follow all instructions until the crisis is resolved.

Prepping to Assist Responders

While emergency personnel are highly trained, they can always use additional assistance from prepared citizens when disaster strikes. Here are ways to properly offer your skills and supplies:

Skills to Volunteer

- Ham radio operating to boost communication abilities
- Search & rescue training to help locate victims
- Construction experience for debris removal
- Medical backgrounds to supplement overwhelmed staff
- Counseling assistance for trauma care

Coordinate with Emergency Services and Authorities
The Ultimate Prepper's Survival Bible

Supply Donations Needed

- Packaged foods and bottled water
- Blankets, cots, camping gear
- Batteries, portable power, lighting
- Basic household goods like toiletries, diapers
- Pet food and supplies

Make sure to coordinate directly with official channels first before self-deploying. Register your offers and get confirmed assignments.

Donations Supply Tracker

Item	Have Qty	Need Qty	Estimated $ Value
Bottled Water	48	-	$24
Energy Bars	20 boxes	-	$100
Blankets	-	20	$160
Batteries	100	200	$150
Solar Charger	1	-	$60

Having a direct line to share your resources makes the emergency response more effective for the community when it's most crucial.

Getting Certified to Assist

To legally operate and assist during emergencies, getting certified training credentials beforehand is wise. Check what official courses cover response skills you can provide.

- **CERT** - Community Emergency Response Team training teaches basic disaster preparedness and response like fire safety and first aid.
- **ARES** - The Amateur Radio Emergency Service licenses you to support backup communication efforts.
- **OCERT** - Organizational/Community Emergency Response Team training provides animal/pet response and management skills.

Bonus Chapter
Communication Strategies

- **Skywarn** - This teaches identifying and reporting severe weather events to assist in forecasting.

Each covers specific areas and provides the proper credentials to get sanctioned for assisting during crises. Research getting certified in any appropriate specialties for you.

Crisis Skills Checklist

Course	Already Certified?	Need Training?
CERT		
ARES		
OCERT		
Skywarn		

The right training makes you an asset rather than a liability when emergencies hit. Your advanced preparations qualify you to integrate seamlessly into the official response efforts.

Bonus
Real-World Case Studies

These true stories show how being prepared in advance - with proper supplies, planning, skills, and practice - can help people safely get through all kinds of scary disasters and crises. Families took smart steps so they were ready when emergencies struck.

Leningrad World War II

When Nazi German forces surrounded and cut off the Russian city of Leningrad (now St. Petersburg), food supplies quickly became desperately scarce for civilians trapped inside the blockaded city.

With supply shortages and starvation setting in, over a million civilians tragically perished during the grueling 900-day siege.

Those who managed to grow small gardens or preserve any little scraps of food available had a better chance of enduring until the siege was finally lifted.

Chilean Miners

In 2010, a mine tunnel caved in while 33 miners worked deep underground in Chile. The miners only had two days of food and water.

This was very dangerous! But the miners knew what to do in emergencies. They rationed out their small supplies very carefully. They set up bathrooms to stay clean. After 17 days, they finally reached the surface with the help of signals.

It took over two more months to get them out! But the prepared miners stayed strong. Their training helped them survive.

Australian Bushfire Incident

In Australia, a huge wildfire burned down many houses, but the Morris family home did not burn down!

That's because the Morris parents had done fire preparation.

They had special fire-proof windows installed.

They cleared any bushes or trees too close to the house. When the fire came, they pumped water from their pool onto their house and yard. The water stopped the flames from burning their home.

Their preparations protected their entire house when others were destroyed.

Bonus Chapter
Communication Strategies

Oklahoma City Bombing

In 1995, terrorists bombed a big office building in Oklahoma City.

Many people got very hurt when part of the building collapsed from the explosion. However, some workers could escape because the building was prepared for bombings. It had strong walls and windows that didn't shatter easily from the blast force.

The workers also knew what to do since they had practiced emergency drills. Their training told them how to evacuate and help anyone injured quickly.

The preparations made the tragic bombing less deadly.

CONCLUSION

Preparedness is not merely a response to potential disasters but a proactive way of life that ensures safety, confidence, and independence. This book has guided you through the necessary steps to make emergency preparedness a seamless part of your daily routine, instilling a sense of security and readiness that goes beyond the individual to embrace the community.

Prepping means more than just buying supplies and taking classes. It is a way of living that makes you self-reliant and responsible. Preppers make smart choices every day to increase their readiness. They pay attention to the news to stay informed about dangers. They learn about possible risks and plan. Preppers stay prepared and not scared by exercising their skills.

It is crucial to have a stock of emergency supplies. However, this means one must be psychologically and physically fit. Feeling like one is ready provides tranquility in the mind. To be able to handle everything is called being confident in yourself. This confidence allows preppers to enjoy life more instead of worrying.

When you prep, you learn how not to rely on anybody. You teach yourself to care for your basic needs such as food, water, housing, security, etc. The sense of depending on oneself that comes with this is liberating and strengthening. Knowledge about one's abilities for survival toughens one up.

Notwithstanding this, preppers do not act out of selfishness or greed. On the contrary, they always intend to protect their families and loved ones from any harm that may come their way. Those who are well prepared should have extra resources available for others in an emergency. Other people can benefit from their talents and knowledge when they face difficult times. The presence of such preparation-prone neighbors improves safety throughout the locality.

A true prepper mentality means taking steps to prevent problems rather than sitting around waiting for them. It's all about taking responsibility for your safety rather than being an innocent prey. Becoming calm under pressure and self-acting – does this make you self-sufficient?

This kind of bravery has been passed down through generations in America. People who settled frontiers had managed through preparation and self-reliance strategies and survived then thrived upon it. By doing so, they honor freedom, self-determination, and overcoming of challenges by their ancestors.Therefore, let these values guide you in embracing education, industry, public strength, and being strong-minded. Accumulate commodities; hone skills regularly; propagate state-of-readiness empowerment; encourage others to do same until it becomes second nature – keep both feet firmly planted on independent reliance but head floating high upon boldness and optimism.

Conclusion

Let the principles of diligence, empowerment, and continuous improvement guide you as you build a life that's not only prepared for the worst but also fully capable of enjoying the best.

And never forget:

"By failing to prepare, you are preparing to fail."

— Benjamin Franklin

BONUS
EXTRA PREPAREDNESS TOOLKIT

Remember that merely stockpiling materials is not enough to be truly prepared. To effectively deal with all sorts of emergencies, you must collect vast amounts of essential information.

Comprehensive Handbook

A complete set of physical and digital materials comprising manuals, books, maps, and references about different survival skills and tactics are crucial equipment for preppers.

- Determine which plants are edible and have medicinal properties.
- Construct dwelling places, snares, utensils, among others.
- Educate yourself on first aid lessons such as CPR and how to handle critical wounds.
- Navigate through maps, compasses, stars etc.
- Make fires using different techniques and materials.
- Preserve food, purify water, and understand basic sanitation.
- Create everyday items using simple, traditional methods.

Having this knowledge at your fingertips allows you to resourcefully apply solutions no matter what gets thrown your way when the chips are down.

Hands-On Training Courses

There's no substitute for gaining true expertise through professional hands-on instruction. Some essential training preppers should look for include:

- Full wilderness survival classes from trusted schools
- Learn about hunting safety and local certifications
- Advanced first aid and emergency medical training
- Learn to use ham radios and set up emergency communications
- Design permaculture systems for growing food independently
- Learn defensive skills such as combat and security

The aim is to become a well-rounded person with a wide range of skills that would enable them

Bonus
Extra Preparedness Toolkit

to succeed even if they had to live without modern technology like people did before factories and machines were common.

Constant Skills Practice

Of course, book knowledge alone isn't enough. Preppers understand the importance of constantly sharpening their abilities through frequent practice by:

- Regularly practicing with unloaded and loaded firearms.
- Use outdoor skills during camping trips to test survival abilities.
- Set up scenarios to practice communicating and being responsible.
- Keep yourself fit with challenging exercise routines.
- Act out stressful situations to prepare for emergencies.
- Learn additional skills apart from the main ones.

Practicing these skills repeatedly helps your body remember them automatically, even when you're feeling stressed and your heart is racing.

Teaching Tomorrow's Survivors

Forward-thinking preppers understand the importance of passing on knowledge to the next generation. They actively involve young children and teenagers by:

- Basic survival skills camps during summer breaks
- Hands-on vocational classes like gardening, animal husbandry, food prep
- First aid, search/rescue, and safety training coursework
- Establish community mentor programs and leadership roles

The goal is to raise cohorts of confident, capable youth resourceful enough to carry the torch of preparedness into an uncertain future where their skills may mean the difference between life and death.

Because at the end of the day, knowledge isn't simply power - it's the supreme survival currency that separates the fragile from the antifragile when the unthinkable happens.

Mutual Defense Arrangements

A strong security team is crucial for protecting the area and monitoring your group's supplies.

Important parts of this include:

- Opt for leaders of great integrity.
- Erect secure core fortresses comprising robust structures.
- Establish safe means of exploration and espionage.
- Develop teams to defend and monitor.
- Assigning definite meeting points for proper organization of all personnel.
- Create explicit regulations on the exercise of violence.

Rule of Law and Justice System

However, community security is not limited to the military. To ensure effective public security, there should be strong policy measures and managerial operations, including:

- Make sure that the rules are understandable and state penalties for breaking them
- Expect to put in place a legal form of custody or imprisonment when needed.
- Determine just manners of punishment and dealing with offenses.
- Solve disputes justly through unbiased community tribunals
- or panels.
- Document everything, provide evidence, and explain any conclusions made.

Continuing Education and Adaptation

Learning survival skills is unlike learning math, where you are done once you master it. With prepping, the education must never stop. There are always new techniques, gear, and threats to study. Preppers stay students for life.

The prepper lessons from this book form a solid start. However, those skills will weaken if you do not practice and review consistently. Set a calendar to regularly test your gear, read through the chapters again, and drill your capabilities. Maybe hold monthly practice missions.

Also, schedule skills training at least once a year. Take a refresher course on wilderness first aid. Attend a new class on finding food in nature or signaling for rescue. Check for updated prepper conventions, meetups, or online courses. Never stop improving your knowledge and abilities.

Gather experience, too, through practice scenarios and simulations. The more high-stress

**Bonus
Extra Preparedness Toolkit**

situations you can simulate, the better your responses will be if real emergencies happen. Embrace small challenges to work out problems.

For example, try living for a week without opening the refrigerator to test your food storage and outdoor cooking skills—camp in the backyard for a few nights to practice living without electricity and running water. Organize neighborhood fire drills to sharpen evacuation timing. The more you stress-test your preps, the better prepared you will become.

Finally, adaptation is crucial as situations change over time. Maybe a new type of disaster risk emerges in your area due to shifts in the climate or escalating wars. Perhaps there are shortages requiring adjustments to your stockpile plans.

Preppers excel at modifying procedures according to changing circumstances. They observe problems, find creative solutions, and overcome obstacles. So follow the news closely, join community prep groups online, and network with other preppers. Collaborating yields good ideas. Shared wisdom keeps everyone learning and improving together.

The goal is to make prepping an ongoing pursuit. There is no "graduation day" when you are finished - only a never-ending cycle of practice, education, and refinement. By continually progressing your readiness, you can remain poised and capable no matter what unexpected events occur.

Facing the Future with Confidence

No one can predict or prevent every emergency. But you can ready yourself with the right skills and gear to feel empowered rather than scared.

There will always be natural disasters, facility breakdowns, conflicts, and other crises that disrupt society. Those risks are unavoidable facts about living on Planet Earth. But you get to decide whether you want to be unprepared and vulnerable or a capable survivor.

By learning and implementing the lessons of this book, you equip yourself with the ability to endure any hardship. From securing clean water to treating wounds to home security and beyond, these skills prepare you to handle chaos.

Self-reliance prevents you from being immobilized by the fear of what is not obvious. You can meet any challenge in days to come because of this training, and should such challenges occur, you have ways of getting through them. Such peace within oneself is beyond any value.

Although disasters might occur, developing resilience and preparedness strategies ensures strong security systems. The emergency unit can let you down, but not for yourself. The supply may fail, but you are stocking up. You feel brave about any problem because you have learned that

Facing the Future with Confidence
The Ultimate Prepper's Survival Bible

you can survive alone without depending on anyone.

This makes individuals confident about facing various challenges, including emergencies. Eliminating vulnerability leads to a heightened sense of positivity. Welcome that happy feeling!

Employ your readiness skills towards daring exploits under the sun, trusting your ability. Go out there and enjoy yourself without any concern. Call upon relatives and friends; then honor your self-reliant way of life.

Above all, let preparedness lift you into wider community involvement. Share what you know so that society can withstand more problems. Be a guide, offering assistance through leadership by lending your helping hand during crises and using the skills that nature has bestowed upon you.

Ultimately, being a prepper is about feeling truly alive. After overcoming the fears and reliance that chain most people down, what else is there but living? Embrace this vibrant self-sovereignty that preparedness provides. Then, walk this earth as a beacon of readiness to inspire others toward brighter futures.

REFERENCES

(2022) 23 tactics for a survival mindset and a positive attitude, Survival Skills Guide. Available at: https://survivalskills.guide/tactics-survival-mindset-positive-attitude/ (Accessed: 29 May 2024).

10 essential medicinal herbs to grow for making home remedies (2021) YouTube. Available at: https://www.youtube.com/watch?v=DZRIzGMr4jE (Accessed: 07 May 2024).

15 natural remedies to soothe a sore throat (no date) Medical News Today. Available at: https://www.medicalnewstoday.com/articles/318631 (Accessed: 17 May 2024).

3 simple steps to store water for emergencies (2023) YouTube. Available at: https://www.youtube.com/watch?v=cCrDs3rf9EM (Accessed: 29 May 2024).

4 ways to make water safe to drink after a disaster (2021) YouTube. Available at: https://www.youtube.com/watch?v=C347hT9lMGQ (Accessed: 29 May 2024).

Aalders, H.C. et al. (2023) Book review: Prepper's long-term survival guide 2nd edition, Knife Magazine. Available at: https://www.knifemagazine.com/book-review-preppers-long-term-survival-guide-2nd-edition/ (Accessed: 29 May 2024).

About survival mindset (no date) Survival Mindset. Available at: https://survivalmindset.us/about/ (Accessed: 29 May 2024).

An unexpected journey: The Power of Financial Preparedness (2023a) YouTube. Available at: https://www.youtube.com/watch?v=pXcjA8UPEiw (Accessed: 16 May 2024).

Apocalypse TV (no date) Google Books. Available at: https://books.google.com.pk/books?hl=en&lr=&id=nunaDwAAQBAJ&oi=fnd&pg=PA113&dq=prepper%2Bmindset&ots=CSmsy7ZLQg&sig=2NZHzt_8CXqIc6tL4_fIm7EHfic&redir_esc=y#v=onepage&q&f=false (Accessed: 29 May 2024).

Avery, S. (2017) Emergency preparedness manuals that don't feel crazy or Make you feel crazy, Medium. Available at: https://medium.com/s/confessions-of-a-left-wing-prepper/confessions-of-a-left-wing-prepper-part-3-63ebe90a0b0 (Accessed: 29 May 2024).

Avery, S. (2017a) Emergency preparedness manuals that don't feel crazy or Make you feel crazy, Medium. Available at: https://medium.com/s/confessions-of-a-left-wing-prepper/confessions-of-a-left-wing-prepper-part-3-63ebe90a0b0 (Accessed: 29 May 2024).

Barker, K. (2020) How to survive the end of the future: Preppers, pathology, and the everyday crisis of insecurity, Transactions (Institute of British Geographers : 1965). Available at: https://www.ncbi.nlm.nih.gov/pmc/articles/PMC7319408/ (Accessed: 29 May 2024).

Barker, K. (2020) How to survive the end of the future: Preppers, pathology, and the everyday crisis of insecurity, Transactions (Institute of British Geographers : 1965). Available at: https://www.ncbi.nlm.nih.gov/pmc/articles/PMC7319408/ (Accessed: 29 May 2024).

Basic emergency plan & family communication plan (no date) Basic Emergency Plan & Family Communication

Plan | Manheim Township, PA - Official Website. Available at: https://www.manheimtownship.org/1107/Basic-Emergency-Plan-Family-Communicatio (Accessed: 20 May 2024).

Be prepared for a financial emergency - ready.gov. Available at: https://www.ready.gov/sites/default/files/2020-03/fema_be-prepared-financial-emergency.pdf (Accessed: 26 May 2024).

Brekke, L., About the Author Laura Brekke The Rev. Laura K. Brekke serves as Benfield-Vick Chaplain at Davis & Elkins College in Elkins and Laura Brekke The Rev. Laura K. Brekke serves as Benfield-Vick Chaplain at Davis & Elkins College in Elkins (2019) Preppers and faith. Available at: https://www.ministrymatters.com/all/entry/9903/preppers-and-faith (Accessed: 29 May 2024).

Building your home herbal medicine cabinet with Amy Hamilton (2016) YouTube. Available at: https://www.youtube.com/watch?v=4OJMETh8mG0 (Accessed: 02 May 2024).

Carson, R. (2022) 10 steps to strengthen your financial emergency preparedness now, Forbes. Available at: https://www.forbes.com/sites/rcarson/2022/09/29/10-steps-to-strengthen-your-financial-emergency-preparedness-now/?sh=6ceb85516ce4 (Accessed: 22 May 2024).

Cities and transport: How global emergencies change the way we move (2021) YouTube. Available at: https://www.youtube.com/watch?v=0L0UIRumgGE (Accessed: 13 May 2024).

Contributor, G. (1970) Health preparedness tips for on-campus life, GradGuard. Available at: https://gradguard.com/blog/health-preparedness-tips-for-on-campus-life/ (Accessed: 05 May 2024).

Creating and storing an emergency water supply (2023) Centers for Disease Control and Prevention. Available at: https://www.cdc.gov/healthywater/emergency/creating-storing-emergency-water-supply.html (Accessed: 29 May 2024).

Crisis communication strategies for emergency and crisis management officials (2023) VCU Wilder Master of Arts in Homeland Security and Emergency Preparedness Online. Available at: https://onlinewilder.vcu.edu/blog/crisis-communication/ (Accessed: 12 May 2024).

Disaster preparedness: Crisis communication plan model (no date) Digital Preservation Management. Available at: https://www.dpworkshop.org/dpm-eng/workshops/management-tools/disaster-preparedness/communication.html (Accessed: 06 May 2024).

Disaster preparedness: Family communications plan (no date) Habitat for Humanity. Available at: https://www.habitat.org/our-work/disaster-response/disaster-preparedness-homeowners/family-communications-plan (Accessed: 21 May 2024).

DIY herbal remedies: Powerful medicinal recipes to try at home (2023) YouTube. Available at: https://www.youtube.com/watch?v=Kho9flCLoUU (Accessed: 17 May 2024).

DIY herbal remedy preparation (2021) YouTube. Available at: https://www.youtube.com/watch?v=wk7vcBumqVo (Accessed: 24 May 2024).

Emergency handbook, UNHCR. Available at: https://emergency.unhcr.org/ (Accessed: 29 May 2024).

Emergency preparedness: Health considerations (2022) YouTube. Available at: https://www.youtube.com/watch?v=9WMJmKH8gGI (Accessed: 11 May 2024).

Emergency public health preparedness | louisvilleky.gov. Available at: https://louisvilleky.gov/government/health-wellness/emergency-public-health-preparedness (Accessed: 27 May 2024).

Emergency public health preparedness | louisvilleky.gov. Available at: https://louisvilleky.gov/government/health-wellness/emergency-public-health-preparedness (Accessed: 23 May 2024).

Escandon, R. (2023) 9 home remedies backed by science, Healthline. Available at: https://www.healthline.com/health/home-remedies (Accessed: 20 May 2024).

Evacuation planning. Available at: https://www.aidr.org.au/media/10352/handbook_evacuation_planning_aidr.pdf (Accessed: 07 May 2024).

Evacuation: Emergency governance and the aesthetics of mobility' by Peter Adey (2022) YouTube. Available at: https://www.youtube.com/watch?v=3qTt-DSaZtQ (Accessed: 01 April 2024).

Events (2014) Preparedness impacts of the changes to health care system financing and delivery infrastructure, The Impacts of the Affordable Care Act on Preparedness Resources and Programs: Workshop Summary. Available at: https://www.ncbi.nlm.nih.gov/books/NBK241389/ (Accessed: 07 May 2024).

Ewan Morrison (2022) The six things I learned from Doomsday prepping, CrimeReads. Available at: https://crimereads.com/the-six-things-i-learned-from-doomsday-prepping/ (Accessed: 29 May 2024).

Financial preparedness in your 20S & 30s (2024) YouTube. Available at: https://www.youtube.com/watch?v=BI9Pp0uBnJM (Accessed: 26 May 2024).

Financial preparedness, Division of Homeland Security and Emergency Services. Available at: https://www.dhses.ny.gov/financial-preparedness (Accessed: 20 May 2024).

Financial preparedness, Get a Game Plan. Available at: https://www.getagameplan.org/make-a-plan/financial-preparedness-tips/ (Accessed: 26 May 2024).

Financial preparedness| Ready.gov. Available at: https://www.ready.gov/financial-preparedness (Accessed: 16 May 2024).

First-aid kits: Stock supplies that can save lives - mayo clinic news network (2015) Mayo Clinic. Available at: https://newsnetwork.mayoclinic.org/discussion/first-aid-kits-stock-supplies-that-can-save-lives/ (Accessed: 29 May 2024).

Flaherty, D.T. (2021) Book review: Preppers long-term survival guide, the starving artist. Available at: https://devontrevarrowflaherty.com/2021/01/14/book-review-preppers-long-term-survival-guide/ (Accessed: 29 May 2024).

Food, M. of A. and (2024) Health and Wellness Preparedness, Province of British Columbia. Available at: https://www2.gov.bc.ca/gov/content/industry/agriservice-bc/health-wellness-preparedness (Accessed: 27 May 2024).

Forum on Medical and Public Health Preparedness for Catastrophic

Frugal living prepping mindset...save money...financial crisis coming (2024) YouTube. Available at:

https://www.youtube.com/watch?v=qMowQ6ziARE (Accessed: 29 May 2024).

Gandhi, Sailaxmi et al. (2021) Psychological preparedness for pandemic (COVID-19) management: Perceptions of nurses and nursing students in India, PloS one. Available at: https://www.ncbi.nlm.nih.gov/pmc/articles/PMC8362956/ (Accessed: 10 May 2024).

Gerson Relocation (2022) Managing emergency situations for global mobility, Gerson Relocation. Available at: https://gersonrelocation.com/global-mobility-emergency-relocation-guide-paper/ (Accessed: 17 May 2024).

Get prepared (no date a) Prepared Housewives. Available at: https://prepared-housewives.com/preppers-long-term-survival-guide-jim-cobb-book-review/ (Accessed: 29 May 2024).

Hall, T. (2023) Health, fitness and emergency preparedness, MyCPR NOW. Available at: https://cprcertificationnow.com/blogs/mycpr-now-blog/health-fitness-and-emergency-preparedness (Accessed: 13 May 2024).

Herbal medicine, Mount Sinai Health System. Available at: https://www.mountsinai.org/health-library/treatment/herbal-medicine (Accessed: 27 May 2024).

Herbal medicine: Types, uses, and safety (no date) Medical News Today. Available at: https://www.medicalnewstoday.com/articles/herbal-medicine (Accessed: 23 May 2024).

Herbs: Deep dive into the world of alternative medicine | community reports (2022) YouTube. Available at: https://www.youtube.com/watch?v=9R194Ypim6o (Accessed: 01 May 2024).

How do we stop relying on 911 to handle mental health crises? | Rand. Available at: https://www.rand.org/pubs/commentary/2023/11/how-do-we-stop-relying-on-911-to-handle-mental-health.html (Accessed: 27 May 2024).

How to cut food waste and maintain food safety. Available at: https://www.fda.gov/media/101389/download (Accessed: 29 May 2024).

How to purify water during a long term disaster (2023) YouTube. Available at: https://www.youtube.com/watch?v=-M_C_Ixva34 (Accessed: 29 May 2024).

Imel-Hartford, L.D., 2013. The Preppers: A Multiple Case Study of Individuals Who Choose a Moderate Survivalist Lifestyle. PhD. Northcentral University. Available at: ProQuest Dissertation & Theses. 3537105.

Industries, B. (2023) Be ready, stay safe: Creating an effective emergency preparedness plan, LinkedIn. Available at: https://www.linkedin.com/pulse/ready-stay-safe-creating-effective-emergency-preparedness/ (Accessed: 10 May 2024).

International Travel Risk Management for student mobility ... Available at: https://teaching.usask.ca/documents/issac/ITRMProceduresGuidelines.pdf (Accessed: 05 May 2024).

Invictus (2022) Developing a prepper mindset for our mental health, Medium. Available at: https://medium.com/@sunflowersutra/developing-a-prepper-mindset-for-our-mental-health-6ea73728b198 (Accessed: 29 May 2024).

James, J.J. (2013) Prevention, preparedness, and wellness: Disaster medicine and public health preparedness, Cambridge Core. Available at: https://www.cambridge.org/core/journals/disaster-medicine-and-public-health-preparedness/article/prevention-preparedness-and-wellness/F39B6377F3B7C0A7C9EF8110FABA91D1 (Accessed: 16 May 2024).

JD_Tuccille (2022) Embrace a bit of prepper mindset for the next emergency-even the government approves, Reason.com. Available at: https://reason.com/2022/09/09/embrace-a-bit-of-prepper-mindset-for-the-next-emergency-even-the-government-approves/ (Accessed: 29 May 2024).

Konstantinovsky. M (2022) Emergency preparedness 101: 4 ways to plan for natural disasters, One Medical. Available at: https://www.onemedical.com/blog/healthy-living/emergency-preparedness-101-4-ways-plan-natural-disasters/ (Accessed: 04 May 2024).

Kylene (2023) How to store water for emergency preparedness - the provident prepper, The Provident Prepper - Common Sense Guide to Emergency Preparedness, Self-Reliance and Provident Living. Available at: https://theprovidentprepper.org/how-to-store-water-for-emergency-preparedness/ (Accessed: 29 May 2024).

MacWelch, T. (2019) Survival skills: 10 Ways to Purify Water, Outdoor Life. Available at: https://www.outdoorlife.com/survival-skills-ways-to-purify-water/ (Accessed: 29 May 2024).

Matheson, C. (1970) Enjoying the heat: Anxiety, fantasy, and doomsday prepping, SpringerLink. Available at: https://link.springer.com/chapter/10.1007/978-3-030-67205-8_8 (Accessed: 29 May 2024).

McAdam, J. (no date) Evacuations: A form of disaster displacement?, Evacuations: a form of disaster displacement? | Forced Migration Review. Available at: https://www.fmreview.org/climate-crisis/mcadam (Accessed: 07 May 2024).

Medicinal herbs: How to make herbal remedies (2020) the herb garden. Available at: https://theherbgarden.ie/using-herbs/medicinal-herbs/ (Accessed: 12 May 2024).

Medicinal plants used as home remedies: A family survey by first year medical students. Available at: https://www.researchgate.net/publication/268282648_Medicinal_Plants_Used_as_Home_Remedies_A_Family_Survey_by_First_Year_Medical_Students (Accessed: 20 May 2024).

Mental health, World Health Organization. Available at: https://www.who.int/news-room/fact-sheets/detail/mental-health-strengthening-our-response/?gad_source=1&gclid=CjwKCAjw9cCyBhBzEiwAJTUWNZTUjMzrx_5N1bMWTp_n3x-YV5JEa5NimYt2_ZIrqEOzlDxNAafRsRoCBCAQAvD_BwE (Accessed: 03 May 2024).

Mobility challenges in times of crises (2022) YouTube. Available at: https://www.youtube.com/watch?v=y72hhiV_zZE (Accessed: 07 May 2024).

Nathan, C. and Hyams, K. (2022) Global policymakers and catastrophic risk, Policy sciences. Available at: https://www.ncbi.nlm.nih.gov/pmc/articles/PMC8637034/ (Accessed: 29 May 2024).

National Preparedness Month encourages preparedness for all types of emergencies (no date) Home. Available at: https://www.fema.gov/press-release/20210318/national-preparedness-month-encourages-preparedness-all-types-emergencies (Accessed: 29 May 2024).

Natural remedies for everyday illnesses (no date) Natural Remedies for Illness | Natural Cures | Allina Health. Available at: https://www.allinahealth.org/healthysetgo/heal/natural-remedies-for-everyday-illnesses (Accessed: 27 May 2024).

New Preparedness plans to respond to emerging major food and nutrition crises (no date) World Bank. Available at: https://www.worldbank.org/en/topic/food-security/brief/countries-catalyze-new-preparedness-plans-to-more-effectively-respond-to-emerging-major-food-and-nutrition-crises (Accessed: 29 May 2024).

Newbie prepper step 5 – water storage and purification (2020) YouTube. Available at: https://www.youtube.com/watch?v=dx1c9PEi_mo (Accessed: 29 May 2024).

Prepper nerd - the fall and resurgence of the prepper mindset - the most impactful influences on the perception of preparedness. Available at: https://prepper-nerd.com/the-fall-and-resurgence-of-the-prepper-mindset-the-most-impactful-influences-on-the-perception-of-preparedness/ (Accessed: 29 May 2024).

Prepper's guide to abundance | survival podcast | prosperity mindset Jack Spirko (2024) YouTube. Available at: https://www.youtube.com/watch?v=ac2sA--EZWE (Accessed: 29 May 2024).

Preventionweb. Available at: https://www.preventionweb.net/files/66345_f357zulchpsychologicalpreparednessf.pdf (Accessed: 26 May 2024).

Psychological first aid for CERT (2021a) YouTube. Available at: https://www.youtube.com/watch?v=qN2MPYCWTXo&list=PL720Kw_OojlJhQgFwWLezJrUpBurbqhHM&index=2 (Accessed: 27 May 2024).

Psychology. Available at: https://psychology.org.au/getmedia/c24bf1ba-a5fc-45d5-a982-835873148b9a/psychological-preparation-for-natural-disasters.pdf (Accessed: 22 May 2024).

Public health emergency preparedness - new haven health (2023) New Haven Health -. Available at: https://nhvhealth.org/emergency-preparedness/ (Accessed: 27 May 2024).

Rainwater harvesting as an alternative water source (2021) Stormwater Solutions. Available at: https://www.stormwater.com/stormwater-bmps/article/33053895/rainwater-harvesting-as-an-alternative-water-source (Accessed: 29 May 2024).

Rainwater harvesting as an alternative water supply in the future. Available at: https://www.researchgate.net/publication/237821822_Rainwater_Harvesting_as_an_Alternative_Water_Supply_in_the_Future (Accessed: 29 May 2024).

Rice, J. (no date) National insecurity: Why do so many in the world's most security conscious nation live in fear?, Digital Commons @ UConn. Available at: https://digitalcommons.lib.uconn.edu/dissertations/1643/ (Accessed: 29 May 2024).

Sacramento ready, Financial Preparedness. Available at: https://sacramentoready.saccounty.gov/Prepare/Pages/financial_preparedness.aspx (Accessed: 11 May 2024).

Samia Richards a et al. (2021) Sustainable water resources through harvesting rainwater and the effectiveness of a low-cost water treatment, Journal of Environmental Management. Available at: https://www.sciencedirect.com/science/article/abs/pii/S0301479721002851 (Accessed: 29 May 2024).

Shelter in emergencies (no date) Humanitarian Coalition. Available at: https://www.humanitariancoalition.ca/shelter-in-emergencies (Accessed: 29 May 2024).

Shelter Safety Handbook some important information on ... Available at: https://www.ifrc.org/sites/default/files/2021-08/305400-Shelter_safety_handbook-EN-LR.pdf (Accessed: 29 May 2024).

Sims, A.A., 2017. Survival of the Preppers: An Exploration into the Culture of Prepping. Ph.D. thesis, University of Missouri - Columbia. Available at: ProQuest Dissertation & Theses. (11012956).

Step 4: How to create a family communication plan for emergencies and Disasters (2024) Primrose Schools. Available at: https://www.primroseschools.com/stories-resources/for-families/step-4-how-to-create-a-family-communication-plan-for-emergencies-and-disasters (Accessed: 26 May 2024).

Survival mindset 101 (2018) Rogue Preparedness - how to get prepared for emergencies and disasters. Available at: https://roguepreparedness.com/survival-mindset-101/ (Accessed: 29 May 2024).

Survival mindset and courses of action. Available at: https://employees.losrios.edu/lrccd/employee/doc/training/training-development-workshop/survival-mindset-presentation.pdf (Accessed: 29 May 2024).

Survival Mindset:5 Keys to navigate any crisis (2021) YouTube. Available at: https://www.youtube.com/watch?v=GtgNwGWsFGw (Accessed: 29 May 2024).

Thompson, B. (2024) Doomsday prepping: Reactionary behavior or inherited instinct? - Seattle psychiatrist, Seattle Anxiety Specialists - Psychiatry, Psychology, and Psychotherapy. Available at: https://seattleanxiety.com/psychiatrist/2023/1/12/doomsday-prepping-reactionary-behavior-or-inherited-instinct (Accessed: 29 May 2024).

Tihk (no date a) Urban survival 101: How to adopt a survival mindset, TIHK. Available at: https://tihk.co/blogs/news/urban-survival-101-how-to-adopt-a-survival-mindset (Accessed: 29 May 2024).

Tribe, M.A. (2022) 6 areas of preparedness, Official Website of the Mescalero Apache Tribe. Available at: https://mescaleroapachetribe.com/16567/6-areas-of-preparedness/ (Accessed: 29 May 2024).

turningpoint82 (2022) Should Christians be doomsday preppers?, David Jeremiah Blog. Available at: https://davidjeremiah.blog/should-christians-be-doomsday-preppers/ (Accessed: 29 May 2024).

UNU-EHS Publication Series - Unu Collections - United ... Available at: http://collections.unu.edu/eserv/UNU:1838/pdf11800.pdf (Accessed: 10 May 2024).

Updated January 18, 2022, Adama, J. and replies, 546 (2022) Best short term emergency water storage, The Prepared. Available at: https://theprepared.com/homestead/reviews/best-two-week-emergency-water-storage-containers/ (Accessed: 29 May 2024).

Urban survival 101: How to adopt a survival mindset, TIHK. Available at: https://tihk.co/blogs/news/urban-survival-101-how-to-adopt-a-survival-mindset (Accessed: 29 May 2024).

Vince Real (no date) Prepper's long term Survival bible, Booktopia. Available at: https://www.booktopia.com.au/prepper-s-long-term-survival-bible-vince-real/book/9789954008027.html (Accessed: 29 May 2024).

Wachtel-Galor, S. (1970b) Herbal medicine, Herbal Medicine: Biomolecular and Clinical Aspects. 2nd edition. Available at: https://ncbi.nlm.nih.gov/books/NBK92773/ (Accessed: 22 May 2024).

We aren't helpless in the face of increasing fires and smoke | Rand. Available at: https://www.rand.org/blog/2023/06/we-arent-helpless-in-the-face-of-increasing-fires-and.html (Accessed: 08 May 2024).

What is your opinion on survivalist and/or prepper mentality? (no date) Quora. Available at: https://www.quora.com/What-is-your-opinion-on-survivalist-and-or-prepper-mentality (Accessed: 29 May 2024).

wikiHow (2023) 3 ways to build a tarp shelter, wikiHow. Available at: https://www.wikihow.com/Build-a-Tarp-Shelter (Accessed: 29 May 2024).

Will the doomsday shelters that have been built withstand all the possible end of days scenarios? (no date) Quora. Available at: https://www.quora.com/Will-the-doomsday-shelters-that-have-been-built-withstand-all-the-possible-end-of-days-scenarios (Accessed: 29 May 2024).

Zulch and Zulch (2019) Psychological preparedness for natural hazards – improving disaster preparedness policy and practice, UNDRR. Available at: https://www.undrr.org/publication/psychological-preparedness-natural-hazards-improving-disaster-preparedness-policy-and (Accessed: 05 May 2024).

GLOSSARY

Activated Charcoal: A substance used to absorb toxins from food poisoning or overdoses.

Air-Tight Room: A sealed-off space within a home used to protect against chemical or biological hazards by preventing outside air infiltration.

Aloe Vera: A plant used to treat burns and promote wound healing.

Ammo cans: Durable, sealable metal containers originally designed for military ammunition storage, commonly repurposed for stashing emergency supplies.

Antenna: A device that transmits and receives radio waves, essential for effective ham radio operation.

ARES: Amateur Radio Emergency Service, a volunteer organization of licensed ham radio operators who assist with emergency communication.

Arnica Cream: A topical treatment for pain, swelling, and bruising from injuries.

Aviation Frequencies: Radio frequencies used for air traffic communication, useful in remote areas.

Backup Water Supplies: Additional water sources kept in reserve to be used during emergencies when normal water supplies are unavailable.

Barter Network: A community of individuals or groups who exchange goods and services without using money.

Bartering: Exchanging goods and services without using money, especially useful in a post-disaster economy.

Basement/Storm Cellar: A designated underground area in a home used for shelter during tornadoes or severe storms.

Basement/underground shelters: Subterranean spaces utilized as refuges from extreme weather or disasters.

Basic maintenance: Routine tasks such as checking fluid levels, tire pressure, and battery condition to keep a vehicle in good working order.

Battery banks: A group of multiple batteries wired together to store and provide backup electrical power.

Battery Packs: Portable power sources used to charge communication devices.

Biodiesel: A renewable fuel made from vegetable oils, animal fats, or recycled cooking greases that can power diesel engines and generators.

Biohazard Bags: Special bags designed to safely contain and dispose of biological waste, preventing the spread of infectious agents.

Biomass: Organic matter like wood, crops, or waste that can be burned to produce heat or converted into biofuels.

Blackberry Root: A plant used as an anti-diarrheal.

Blinding Flashlights: Portable lights with intense brightness or strobing effects used to disorient potential attackers.

Bottle Filters/Straws: Portable water filtration systems integrated into bottles or straws, allowing direct filtration during drinking.

Brine: A solution of salt and water used for pickling and fermenting foods.

Bugout backpack: A bag packed with essential survival items for use during an emergency evacuation.

Bug-out bag (BOB): A portable kit containing essential survival items that can be easily grabbed and carried during an evacuation.

Bugout location (BOL): A predetermined safe location where preppers plan to retreat or evacuate during an emergency or disaster.

Bushcraft: Skills for surviving in priminitive wilderness settings through fire-craft, toolmaking, shelter building, etc.

Calendula: An annual herb used to make healing salves.

Camouflage: Materials or patterns used to blend in with the surrounding environment and avoid detection.

Camouflage: Methods and materials for concealing one's presence visually from detection.

Canned Fruit/Vegetable Juices: Packaged beverages derived from fruits or vegetables, potentially serving as a source of hydration during emergencies.

Canning/Dehydrating/Smoking: Methods of preserving foods like fruits, vegetables, and meats for long-term storage.

Canning: A method of preserving food by packing it into jars or cans and heating it to kill microorganisms.

Case lot sales: Retailer discounts offered for purchasing entire case/shipping quantities of grocery items.

Cayenne Tincture: A concentrated extract used to stop bleeding and increase circulation.

CB Radio: A type of radio used for short- to medium-range communication, requiring a CB license.

CERT: Community Emergency Response Team, a program that trains volunteers for disaster response.

Chain of command: A strict hierarchy and ranks used to structure decision-making authority and leadership roles.

Chamomile: A plant used to reduce inflammation and aid sleep.

Charge controllers: Regulators used in solar and wind power systems to prevent batteries from overcharging and ensure efficient charging.

Coded messages: Pre-arranged signals or phrases used to communicate discreetly.

Cognitive behavioral therapy: A psychotherapy that modifies dysfunctional thought patterns and behaviors.

Cold water misters: Devices that spray a fine mist of water to provide evaporative cooling.

Command Center: A centralized location in a home or community equipped with communication tools and emergency supplies.

Communication/navigation devices: Tools such as phones, radios, and GPS devices used to stay informed and find your way during an evacuation.

Compass: A navigational instrument with a magnetized needle for determining cardinal directions.

Contingency plan: A backup plan to be used if the original plan fails or conditions change.

Cooling vests: Wearable garments with inserts that can be frozen or filled with water to keep the body cool.

Corydalis: A plant with numbing and anti-inflammatory properties for nerve pain.

CPR: Cardiopulmonary resuscitation, an emergency procedure that combines chest compressions and artificial ventilation to maintain blood circulation and breathing.

Crampbark: A plant used as an antispasmodic for cramps and muscle spasms.

Creative Outlets: Activities like arts and crafts that boost morale and positivity.

Creative Signaling: Alternative methods like messenger pigeons, signal mirrors, or smoke signals used to communicate when modern technology fails.

Crisis Scenario: A hypothetical situation used to illustrate coping strategies and actions.

Dams: Barriers constructed across rivers or streams to control water flow and create reservoirs for hydroelectric power generation.

Debt Consolidation: Combining multiple debts into one payment to simplify management and potentially reduce interest rates.

Debt Repayment Plan: A strategy for paying off debts, prioritizing high-interest debts to reduce financial burden.

Decoction: A preparation method where tough plant parts are simmered to extract medicinal compounds.

Deep cycle batteries: Lead-acid batteries designed to be regularly deeply discharged and recharged for energy storage applications.

Dehydrating: Removing moisture from foods to extend their shelf life.

Dehydrator: A small kitchen appliance that removes moisture from foods through a heated venting process to enable long-term storage.

Dental Kits: Prepackaged sets containing tools and materials for temporary dental care.

Devil's Claw: A plant with anti-inflammatory properties for arthritis and back pain.

Draft-proofed: Sealing leaks and gaps in buildings to prevent uncontrolled air flow and heat transfer.

Drain Pipes: Pipes installed around the exterior of a building to redirect water away from the foundation and prevent flooding.

Dry Shampoo: A powder or spray used to clean hair without water, suitable for use in situations where bathing is not possible.

Echinacea (Coneflower): A plant that boosts immunity and fights infections.

Economic Impact of a Crisis: The effects of a disaster on the economy, including job losses, inflation, and supply chain disruptions.

Elderberry: A plant used to fight viruses and clear mucus, often in syrup form.

Electrical system backups: Alternative power sources and solutions to ensure a vehicle's electrical systems function during an emergency.

Emergency bivvy: A lightweight, portable shelter designed for emergency use to provide warmth and protection.

Emergency Blanket: A compact, lightweight blanket designed to retain body heat and provide warmth in emergency situations.

Emergency Broadcasts: Radio or TV transmissions that provide critical information during crises.

Emergency communications: Systems and devices used to relay information during a crisis.

Emergency First Aid Supplies: Essential items needed to provide immediate medical care in emergency situations.

Emergency Frequencies: Specific radio frequencies designated for emergency communication.

Emergency Fund: Savings set aside to cover essential expenses during financial emergencies.

Emergency kit: A collection of supplies and tools kept in your vehicle or home to assist during an emergency.

Emergency officials: Authorities responsible for managing and coordinating responses during crises.

Emergency Operations Center: A central facility that coordinates emergency response efforts and communication.

Emergency services: Official response agencies like ambulance, fire, and police departments.

Emergency Sheltering: The act of seeking refuge in a secure location within one's home during hazardous situations such as severe weather or civil unrest.

Emergency supplies: Items like water, food, clothing, medications, and hygiene products prepared for use during an evacuation.

Emergency Water Collection: The immediate gathering of water from available sources during crises, ensuring access to essential hydration.

Environmental survival: Techniques and skills for staying alive in various outdoor settings and conditions.

Essential Expenses: Basic living costs such as housing, food, utilities, and transportation.

Evacuation route: A pre-planned path to exit your neighborhood or city in case of an emergency.

Evacuation: An organized withdrawal from a dangerous area to an area of safety.

Evaporative coolers: Air conditioners that cool air through the evaporation of water, ideal for dry climates.

Everyday Carry (EDC): Essential items that preppers carry on their person at all times, such as a multi-tool, flashlight, and first aid kit.

Faraday cage: An enclosure made of conductive material used to block electromagnetic fields and protect electronic devices from electromagnetic pulses (EMPs).

Fennel: A plant used for cramp and gas relief.

Fermentation: A process in which microorganisms like bacteria or yeast convert carbohydrates into alcohols or acids used for food preservation.

Feverfew: A perennial herb used for natural headache relief.

Fieldcraft: Various techniques and skills for operating and surviving in rural environments and rough terrain.

Financial Preparedness: The practice of planning and organizing your finances to ensure stability during crises.

Fire drills: Practice evacuation exercises simulating how to safely exit a building if there is a fire emergency.

Fireplace inserts: Wood-burning units designed to fit inside an existing fireplace to improve heating efficiency.

First aid procedures: Established techniques to provide initial care for injuries or illnesses.

First Aid: Immediate care provided to a sick or injured person until professional medical help arrives.

Foraging: The act of searching for and collecting wild plants for food or medicinal purposes.

Foraging: The act of searching for and gathering food from the wild.

Foundation: The structural base of a building, including walls and footings, upon which the rest of the structure rests.

Freeze-dried food buckets: Large rigid pails containing freeze-dried, shelf-stable food rations designed for long-term storage.

Freeze-dried meals: Pre-packaged meals with the moisture removed through a freeze-drying process for long-term preservation.

FRS: Family Radio Service, a low-power radio service for short-distance communication without a license.

Garlic: A quick-growing plant with antiviral and antibacterial properties.

Generators: Machines that convert mechanical energy into electrical energy, often powered by fuel sources like gasoline, propane, or natural gas.

Ginger: A plant used to ease nausea and reduce muscle pain.

Glossary:

GMRS: General Mobile Radio Service, a licensed radio service for communication over medium distances.

Go-bag: A pre-packed bag containing essential items needed for quick evacuation.

Goggles: Protective eyewear that shields the eyes from liquids, debris, and other hazards.

Gravity Filters: Water filtration systems that utilize gravity to slowly pass water through a filter, resulting in purified water.

Gray man: The ability to blend in and avoid unwanted attention in a survival situation.

Ground-coupled heat pumps: HVAC systems that use the constant temperature of the Earth for heating and cooling buildings.

Groundwater: Water located beneath the earth's surface, often accessed by digging wells or other methods for extraction.

Ham Radio License: Certification required to legally operate a ham radio, issued by the FCC.

Ham Radio: A global communication device operated by licensed amateur radio enthusiasts.

Hand-crank radio: A battery-less radio powered by a hand-operated crank mechanism for situations without electricity.

Hands-On Training: Practical instruction and practice sessions aimed at developing proficiency in self-defense skills.

Hardship Program: Payment relief options offered by creditors during financial crises.

Headlamps: Portable light sources worn on the head, allowing hands-free illumination and visibility.

Heat stroke: A life-threatening condition caused by the body overheating, requiring immediate cooling.

Herbal Medicine: Natural remedies derived from plants used to treat various health conditions.

Herbal Remedies: Treatments made from medicinal plants, used as an alternative or complement to conventional medicine.

High-Value Barter Items: Goods that are in high demand during a crisis, such as non-perishable food, water, and tools.

Hip waders: Waterproof overalls worn to prevent oversaturation when standing in deep water.

Holly Berries: Berries used to reduce fever.

Homesteading: Living a self-sufficient lifestyle, often involving gardening, canning, and animal husbandry.

Homesteading: The practice of self-sufficient living, often involving activities like gardening, animal husbandry, and food preservation.

Homesteading: The self-sufficient practice of operating a small farm or residence producing food, livestock, and energy.

Horehound: A plant with cough suppressant and expectorant properties.

Hot Water Heater Tanks: Containers storing heated water for household use, which can be utilized as an alternative water source during emergencies.

HVAC: Acronym for heating, ventilation, and air conditioning systems used to regulate indoor environmental conditions.

Hydroelectric: Relating to the production of electricity by the force of flowing water turning turbines.

Hygiene: Practices that promote cleanliness and prevent the spread of illness and disease.

Impact-Resistant Shingles: Roofing materials engineered to withstand high winds and impact from debris during severe weather.

Infusion: A method where soft plant parts are steeped in hot water to extract beneficial properties.

Insulated coverall suits: One-piece, full-body insulated garments that cover from head-to-toe in extreme cold conditions.

Insulation: Materials used to prevent heat transfer and reduce energy costs for heating/cooling.

Inverters: Devices that convert the direct current (DC) electricity produced by solar panels or batteries into alternating current (AC) that can power ordinary household appliances.

Jamaica Dogwood: A pain tonic used in the Caribbean for various aches and pains.

Jerky: Lean meat trimmed, seasoned, and dehydrated into a shelf-stable product.

Kimchi: A traditional Korean dish of fermented vegetables, usually cabbage, with various seasonings.

Knot-tying: The formation of knot patterns in ropes for purposes like binding, lashing, climbing, etc.

Land navigation: Using maps, compasses and terrain features to plan routes and determine directions overland.

Larder: A cool room or pantry where food is stored.

Latex Gloves: Disposable gloves made of latex, worn to maintain a sterile field during medical procedures.

Laughter is the Best Medicine: The therapeutic benefits of humor in difficult circumstances.

Lavender Oil: An oil used as a disinfectant and for calming burns and sleep issues.

Lavender: A versatile perennial herb with medicinal flowers.

LED lights: Highly energy-efficient lighting that uses light-emitting diodes to produce illumination while consuming minimal power.

Licorice Root: A plant used for overall gut healing and soothing the digestive system.

Litters/Stretchers: Portable devices used for lifting and carrying patients, providing support during transport.

Lobelia: A plant that helps relax bronchial spasms during asthma attacks.

Marine VHF: A radio service used for communication on waterways.

Marshmallow Root: A plant used for intestinal wellness and soothing the digestive tract.

Mediators: Trusted individuals or committees that oversee and resolve disputes within a barter network.

Medicinal Plants: Plants that contain substances beneficial for healing and health improvement.

Messenger Pigeons: Trained birds that carry messages over long distances.

Micro-hydroelectric systems: Small-scale hydropower systems that generate electricity by capturing the energy of flowing water to spin turbines.

Mind Over Matter: Mental strength and mindset in overcoming challenges.

Mindfulness: The practice of being present and accepting of one's thoughts and feelings.

Mint: A perennial herb that helps with stomach and nausea issues.

Mullein: A plant used as a respiratory tonic to soothe inflammation and coughs.

Multiple Income Streams: Having several sources of income to increase financial stability and security.

MURS: Multi-Use Radio Service, a license-free two-way radio service for business and personal use.

Mylar bags: Bags made of mylar (a versatile plastic sheeting material) for moisture and air-proof food storage.

Natural gas: A gaseous fossil fuel mixture, primarily methane, used for heating homes and generating electricity.

Navigation (map/compass): Orienting one's position and planned routes using maps and compasses.

NOAA Weather Radio: A type of radio that broadcasts continuous weather information and emergency alerts.

Non-Lethal Defense: Defensive tools and devices designed to incapacitate or deter attackers without causing permanent harm or injury.

Non-perishable food: Food items that have a long shelf life and do not require refrigeration.

Obstetrical Kit: A package containing sterile tools and supplies for assisting with childbirth.

Off-grid: Living independently and self-sufficiently, without reliance on public utilities or services.

Off-road capabilities: Enhancements and features that enable a vehicle to travel on rough or unpaved terrain.

Operational security (OPSEC): The practice of protecting sensitive information and activities from potential adversaries or threats.

Oral Anesthetic Gels: Topical gels used to numb mouth pain caused by toothaches or oral sores.

Outhouse: A simple outdoor toilet structure, often dug into the ground, used when indoor plumbing is unavailable.

Pain relievers: Medications, often over-the-counter, that help alleviate bodily aches and pains.

Passive cooling: Methods of cooling buildings or spaces without using energy-intensive air conditioning, such as shading, ventilation, or burying underground.

Passive Income: Earnings from investments or businesses that do not require active involvement.

Pathology diagnosis: Identifying the nature of diseases and injuries by evaluating symptoms/signs.

Patient Drags: Harnesses or straps designed for pulling an injured person across terrain.

Pedestrian evacuation: The process of leaving an area on foot due to an emergency when vehicles are not an option.

Pemmican: A concentrated food made of dried lean meat mixed with fat, used by Native Americans and early explorers.

Peppermint: A plant used to relieve digestive issues.

Permaculture: A sustainable design system that aims to create self-sufficient and resilient agricultural ecosystems.

Permaculture: An agricultural approach focused on sustainable food production by mimicking natural ecosystems.

Personal Security Alarms: Devices that emit loud sounds to attract attention and deter attackers during emergencies.

Pet Water Storage: Reserved water supplies specifically allocated for pets' hydration needs during emergencies, ensuring their health and well-being

Photovoltaic panels: Panels made up of multiple solar cells that convert sunlight directly into electricity through the photovoltaic effect.

PLB: Personal Locator Beacon, a device that transmits your location to search and rescue teams.

Portable Mesh Network: A temporary internet network created without traditional infrastructure.

Portable Radios: Battery-operated radios for receiving broadcasts and communicating.

Portable Shower: A portable device used for bathing when traditional facilities are unavailable, often using stored water.

Portable Water Filters: Compact filtration systems designed for easy transport and use, often utilized during outdoor activities or emergencies.

Positive Mindset: An optimistic outlook that helps in facing adversity.

Potable water: Water that is safe to drink.

Poultice: A paste made from fresh herbs applied directly to the skin or wounds.

Powdered milk/eggs: Dehydrated dairy and egg products in powder form that can be rehydrated for cooking and baking.

Power walls: Rechargeable battery packs that store electricity from solar panels or the grid for powering homes.

Power-saving measures: Techniques and devices to reduce electricity consumption, like energy-efficient appliances.

Preplanned meeting spot: A designated safe location predetermined for all family members to congregate at in case of an emergency evacuation.

Prepper: A person who prepares for emergencies or disasters by stockpiling supplies and learning survival skills.

Primary evacuation route: The main pre-planned path for leaving an area during an emergency.

Primitive hunting: Basic methods of hunting using simple tools like bows, spears, or slingshots.

Probiotics: Live bacteria and yeasts that are beneficial for human health, especially digestive health, found in fermented foods.

Propane: A flammable hydrocarbon gas commonly used as a portable fuel for heating and powering generators.

Psychological Preparedness: Being mentally and emotionally ready to face challenging situations.

Pump Filters: Filtration devices equipped with a hand pump mechanism to force water through the filter, effectively removing impurities.

Purification Methods: Techniques employed to make water safe for drinking by removing contaminants, pathogens, or impurities.

RACES: Radio Amateur Civil Emergency Service, a radio service for emergency communications.

Radio Telephone Interconnect: A system that connects radios to telephone networks for extended communication capabilities.

Radio Watch Program: A schedule of volunteers monitoring radio frequencies for emergency updates and communication.

Rainwater Harvesting: Collection and storage of rainwater for later use, typically through the use of containers placed outdoors.

Rally point: A designated meeting place along an evacuation route where family members can reunite if separated.

Rations: A fixed amount of food or provisions, especially for soldiers or during emergencies.

Reasonable Use of Force Laws: Legal guidelines dictating when and how much force is justifiable in self-defense situations.

Renewable energy systems: Power sources that harness renewable natural energy flows like sunlight, wind, water, etc.

Repeater: A device that receives and retransmits radio signals to extend their range.

Reservoirs: Artificially created lakes or ponds for storing water to be utilized in hydroelectric power plants.

Resilience: The ability to bounce back from difficult experiences.

Resuscitation: The act of reviving someone from unconsciousness or apparent death.

Rigid Splints: Stiff devices used to immobilize a body part or stabilize a fracture during transportation.

Roof rakes: Long-handled rakes or scrapers used to remove snow and ice accumulation from rooftops.

Root cellaring: A traditional method of storing root vegetables in an excellent, humid underground space or basement.

Root cellars: Underground storage chambers for keeping foods like vegetables and fruits fresh for extended periods.

Safe Room: A fortified interior space within a home designed to provide protection from intruders or dangerous events.

Safety masks: Protective face coverings that filter out smoke, dust, and other particulates from the air you breathe.

Safety whistle: A high-pitched whistle, often on a lanyard, used for signaling for help when in distress.

Salve: An ointment made by infusing herbs into oils and mixing with beeswax.

Sanitation (latrines): Designated facilities and methods for the safe, sanitary disposal of human waste.

Sanitation: Measures taken to maintain a clean and healthy environment, including waste disposal and hygiene practices.

Sanitization: The act of cleaning and disinfecting storage containers or surfaces to ensure water safety and prevent contamination.

Sanitizing Solution: A solution containing disinfectants used to kill germs and bacteria, often used for cleaning surfaces and equipment.

Satellite Phone: A phone that uses satellites for communication, functioning globally.

Sauerkraut: Finely shredded cabbage that lactic acid bacteria have fermented.

Scurvy: A disease caused by a deficiency of vitamin C, characterized by bleeding gums, tooth loss, and weakness.

Search/rescue: Operations to locate and retrieve people in distress or danger, often in wilderness settings.

Secondary evacuation route: An alternative path used if the primary route is blocked or unsafe.

Security System: A comprehensive set of devices and measures designed to protect a home from intrusion or emergencies.

Self-defense items: Tools or weapons carried to protect oneself during an emergency.

Self-Defense Techniques: Strategies and tools used to protect oneself from harm, including non-lethal methods and physical skills.

Self-Sufficiency Practices: Activities that reduce reliance on external sources, such as gardening or basic home repairs.

Shelter systems: Portable temporary structures like tents designed to provide basic shelter in emergencies.

Shortwave receiver: A radio capable of receiving international broadcasts, often used for emergency communication.

Side Income: Additional money earned outside of your primary job, such as through freelance work or a small business.

Signal Mirrors: Devices used to reflect sunlight and send visual signals over distances.

Signaling equipment: Devices like mirrors, whistles, etc. used to attract attention or convey distress signals.

Siphon gas: The process of transferring fuel from one vehicle or container to another.

Situational awareness: Active monitoring of one's environment to maintain heightened alertness of potential threats.

Skywarn: A program that trains individuals to recognize and report severe weather conditions to aid forecasting.

Slippery Elm Bark: A plant used to treat wounds and soothe the digestive tract.

Smart power strips: Power strips that automatically cut power to devices not in use to prevent energy waste.

Smoke Signals: A method of sending coded messages using smoke puffs.

Smokehouses: Small enclosed buildings used for smoking and curing meats as a preservation technique.

Solar arrays: A complete setup of multiple solar panels connected together to generate solar power.

Solar attic fans: Roof-mounted fans powered by solar panels that draw hot air out of attics to reduce cooling needs.

Solar power bank: A rechargeable battery pack that stores electricity generated by integrated solar panels.

Solar radio: A radio that runs on electricity generated by built-in solar panels, providing power without batteries.

Solar still: A device that uses sunlight to distill fresh water from salty or contaminated water.

Spark Arrestors: Devices fitted to chimneys and vents to prevent sparks and embers from escaping and causing fires.

Splint Padding: Material used to cushion and protect pressure points when applying a splint.

Splint: A device used to immobilize and protect an injured limb or body part.

Splinting materials: Rigid devices like metal or plastic splints used to immobilize and stabilize injured limbs.

Stoic philosophies: A school of Hellenistic philosophy that promoted virtues like resilience and self-control.

Storm Shutters: Permanent coverings installed over windows and doors to protect them from wind, rain, and flying debris during storms.

Supply caches: Stockpiles or hidden stashes of vital emergency supplies and equipment in reserve locations.

Supply Chain Disruptions: Interruptions in the process of producing and distributing goods, often leading to shortages.

Support Network: Family, friends, and community groups that provide assistance and emotional support.

Sustainment: The provisions and resources required to maintain operations without interruption long-term.

Swimming Pools/Hot Tubs: Artificial bodies of water commonly found in residential settings, requiring purification before use as drinking water.

TEOTWAWKI (The End Of The World As We Know It): A term used to describe a catastrophic event that leads to the collapse of modern civilization.

Terrain: The physical features and characteristics of the landscape.

Thermal blocking: Insulation techniques that reflect heat to reduce the energy required for heating and cooling.

Thermal jackets: Heavily insulated cold-weather outerwear designed to trap body heat and prevent heat loss.

Tincture: A concentrated extract made by soaking plants in alcohol.

Trading: The act of buying, selling, or exchanging goods and services, which can become crucial when traditional financial systems fail.

Trapping: The method of capturing animals for food using traps or snares.

Triage: The process of determining the priority of patients' treatments based on the severity of their condition.

Turbine blades: The aerodynamic blades attached to turbines that spin when exposed to a moving fluid like water or wind.

Umbilical Clamps: Medical clamps used to secure the umbilical cord after birth.

Vacuum sealing: A technique for removing air from a package or container used to extend the shelf life of foods.

Valerian: A perennial herb used as a sleep aid and calming agent.

Valuation System: A method for determining the value of goods and services in a barter system, ensuring fair trade.

Vehicle preparedness: The state of having your vehicle ready and equipped for emergency evacuations.

Vent Covers: Protective covers installed over vents and chimneys to prevent debris, animals, and weather elements from entering.

Ventilation: The movement of air in and out of a space to circulate fresh air and remove stale air.

Walkie-Talkies: Handheld two-way radios for short-distance communication.

Water bath canning: A method of preserving food by submerging sealed jars in boiling water for a specific time.

Water filter/purifier: A device used to remove impurities and make water safe for drinking.

Water purification systems: Methods and devices used to remove contaminants and make non-potable water safe for drinking.

Water Purification Tablets: Chemical tablets containing substances like chlorine or iodine, used to disinfect and purify water for safe consumption.

Water purifier: A portable device that uses filters or other means to remove contaminants and make non-potable water safe for drinking.

Water Rotation: The practice of systematically using and replenishing stored water supplies to maintain freshness and quality over time.

Water Storage Plan: A systematic strategy outlining the methods and locations for storing water to ensure availability during emergencies.

Weapon Laws: Regulations governing the possession, use, and storage of firearms and other weapons in a specific area.

Weatherizing Sealants: Protective coatings applied to surfaces to prevent water infiltration and damage from weather elements.

White Willow Bark: A natural pain reliever containing salicin, similar to aspirin.

Wild Cherry Bark: A natural cough suppressant and decongestant.

Wild edible plants: Plants that can be safely consumed, found in natural environments.

Wilderness navigation: The skills for finding one's way and traveling safely through undeveloped, remote areas.

Willow Bark: A natural source of salicin, used for pain relief similar to aspirin.

Wind farms: An area with a group of wind turbines installed to capture wind energy and generate electricity.

Wind turbines: Machines with large blades that spin when blown by wind, capturing the wind's kinetic energy and converting it into electricity via generators.

Window tinting: Applying treated glazing or films to windows to reduce heat gain from sunlight.

Wood gasifiers: Systems that convert solid biomass fuels like wood chips or pellets into combustible gases to run generators or engines.

Wood stoves: Enclosed heating appliances that burn wood fuel to provide warmth through radiant heat transfer.

Wood-burning stove: An enclosed heating appliance that burns wood fuel to provide warmth and heating capability.

Yarrow: A plant used for stopping bleeding and treating wounds.

Printed in Great Britain
by Amazon